A COMPREHENSIVE GUIDE TO WELLNESS IN LAW

SIR JAMES GRAY ROBINSON, ESQ.

AMERICAN BAR ASSOCIATION
Family Law Section

Cover design by Sara Wadford/ABA Design

Printed in the United States of America.

28 27 26 25 24   5 4 3 2 1

Library of Congress Cataloging-in-Publication Data

Names: Robinson, James Gray, author. | American Bar Association. Section of Family Law, issuing body.
Title: A comprehensive guide to wellness in law / Sir James Gray Robinson, Esq.
Description: 1st edition. | Chicago : American Bar Association, Section of Family Law, 2024. | Includes index. | Summary: "In the legal profession, the pursuit of justice often comes at a cost-a toll on the mental health and well-being of lawyers. Burnout, depression, and elevated rates of anxiety are critical issues affecting the legal community. Recent studies from Massachusetts and California/District of Columbia reveal alarming statistics, shedding light on the mental health challenges within the profession. I am not writing this book as an academic exercise. In 2004, at the height of my legal career, I had a nervous breakdown and quit practicing law. I was a third-generation trial lawyer in North Carolina, AV rated in the Martindale-Hubbell law directory by my peers. I had many friends and colleagues. Yet, despite doing everything "right," I was hiding a dark secret which nearly destroyed my soul. I was desperately unhappy, wrestling with demons, PTSD, and addiction. I looked to alternative medical practices to heal myself. I had been in conventional "talk" therapy for years, but it wasn't even scratching the surface of the demons of my past, my obesity, my exhaustion, and my shame. I felt something new was required to heal my deep-seated issues, and I found it in alternative medicine and coaching. I am writing this book to share a message of hope and redemption for all lawyers struggling with stress, anxiety, depression, or addiction. I have survived all those issues and want to guide you to the resilience you need to achieve happiness, satisfaction, confidence, and success. The identities of the lawyers that are discussed here have been changed to protect privacy, but the symptoms and the results are real"-- Provided by publisher.
Identifiers: LCCN 2024012820 | ISBN 9781639055050 (paperback) | ISBN 9781639055067 (epub)
Subjects: LCSH: Practice of law--United States. | Lawyers--United States. | Happiness--United States. | Spiritual life.
Classification: LCC KF300 .R59 2024 | DDC 340.023/73--dc23/eng/20240325
LC record available at https://lccn.loc.gov/2024012820

ISBN 978-1-63905-505-0

Discounts are available for books ordered in bulk. Special consideration is given to state bars, CLE programs, and other bar-related organizations. Inquire at Book Publishing, ABA Publishing, American Bar Association, 321 N. Clark Street, Chicago, Illinois 60654-7598.

www.shopABA.org

Contents

Foreword vii
About the Author xi
Introduction xiii

1 Unmasking the Hidden Struggles: The State of Lawyer Well-Being 1

1.1 The Burnout Epidemic: A Legal Crisis 3
1.2 Anxiety and Depression: Uninvited Companions 5
1.3 Suicidal Thoughts: A Cry for Help 10
1.4 The Source of Stress 12
1.5 Overwhelm 13

2 The Legal Profession's Silent Sufferers: Unraveling the Mental Health Crisis 15

2.1 The High-Pressure Environment: An Incubator for Mental Struggles 15
2.2 The Perfectionist's Dilemma: Striving for the Unattainable 16
2.3 The Silent Stigma: Mental Health Taboos in the Legal World 21
A. The Fear of Perceived Weakness 23
B. The "Always-On" Culture 25

C. Fear of Professional Consequences 27
D. The "Suck It Up" Culture 29
E. Fear of Perceived Judgment 31
F. Lack of Education and Awareness 34
2.4 The Isolated Practitioner: Loneliness in the Legal Landscape 35
2.5 The Call for Change: Embracing Mental Health as a Priority 36

3 Addiction and Law 41

3.1 Alcohol's Effect on the Brain 42
3.2 Alcohol's Effect on the Body 43

4 The Path to Resilience: Cultivating Mental Strength in the Legal Profession 45

4.1 Understanding Resilience: The Power to Bounce Back 48
4.2 Building Mental Resilience: Strategies for Lawyers 55
4.3 Embracing Emotional Intelligence: Navigating the Legal Terrain 69
A. Establish Who You Want to Represent 73
B. Have a Plan 74
C. Be Honest with Yourself 74
D. Establish Your Priorities 74
E. Find Your Voice 75
F. Build and Maintain a Rapport 75
G. Find Your Platform 75
H. Don't Quit 76
I. How to Feel in Control 76
J. Be Your Best 76
4.4 Cultivating Resilience in Legal Organizations 82

5 The Power of Self-Care: Nurturing Well-Being in the Legal Profession 87

5.1 Understanding Self-Care: A Vital Component of Resilience 87
5.2 The Pillars of Self-Care: Strategies for Lawyers 94
A. Managing Workload and Boundaries 94
B. The Power of Mindful Awareness 95
1. Ho'oponopono 100
2. Vagus Nerve 103
3. Hakalau 104
4. Meditation 105
5. Health Is Wealth 108
6. Strength in Connections 110
7. Spirituality for Lawyers 110
8. Set Your Daily Goals 114
9. Be Like Buddha 116
10. Dealing with Unpleasant Lawyers 120
5.3 Redefining Success: A Paradigm Shift for Lawyers 123
5.4 Embracing the Journey to Self-Care 124

6 Fostering a Supportive Legal Community: Building a Culture of Well-Being 133

6.1 The Strength of Connection: Creating a Supportive Network 133
6.2 Challenging the Stigma: Opening the Dialogue on Mental Health 134
6.3 Advocating for Work–Life Integration: Redefining Legal Workspaces 135
6.4 Promoting Leadership in Well-Being 135
6.5 A Call for Collaboration: A Collective Responsibility 136

6.6 The ABA Pledge and Expectations 136
6.7 A Radical Idea 137
A. Mentors 137
B. Involve Family 138
C. Involve Colleagues 138

Conclusion: Thriving Together, A Journey of Resilience, Self-Care, and Support 139
Endnotes 141

Appendix Affirmations 151

Index 163

Foreword

In the demanding world of law, where stress is an unwelcome companion in every courtroom and law office, *A Comprehensive Guide to Wellness in Law* emerges as a vital companion for attorneys seeking refuge from the relentless pressures of legal practice. Authored by Sir James Gray Robinson, Esq., a seasoned practitioner turned advocate for attorney wellness, this book is a well-researched beacon of insight and guidance, inviting legal professionals on a transformative journey toward balance, resilience, and a fulfilling legal career.

As the director of the Lawyers and Judges Assistance Program for the past 5 years, mental health clinician for over 20 years, and the daughter of a lawyer with over four decades of practice, I believe Mr. Robinson brings a unique perspective to the challenges faced by attorneys, judges, and legal professionals. Having experienced the profound impact of stress firsthand, the author advocates for a collective shift toward prioritizing mental and physical health in the legal community.

Mr. Robinson's dual role as a former practicing attorney and a dedicated coach to legal professionals adds a rich layer of authenticity to the narrative. Drawing from personal experiences and the stories of those he has coached over the years, this book provides real-life examples that resonate with the struggles and frustrations familiar to anyone navigating the legal landscape.

This book doesn't just acknowledge the issues; it offers practical strategies to foster resilience and combat the challenges inherent in legal practice. With a keen understanding of the multifaceted nature of stress in the legal profession, Mr. Robinson encourages readers to reflect on their thinking patterns and challenges them to consider new perspectives.

A Comprehensive Guide to Wellness in Law is more than a book; it's a toolkit for attorneys seeking to transform their professional lives. By presenting various options to address individual circumstances, the author recognizes that there is no one-size-fits-all solution to the personal challenges faced by legal professionals. The book serves as a valuable resource, offering actionable insights and encouraging readers to tailor their approach to wellness.

As a practitioner who discusses many of the book's suggestions in continuing legal education (CLE) seminars, I appreciate its resourcefulness and relevance to the ongoing conversation about attorney well-being. *A Comprehensive Guide to Wellness in Law* is an indispensable guide for legal professionals at all stages of their careers, providing the support needed to navigate the complexities of the legal field while prioritizing personal wellness. In these pages, discover the power of balance, resilience, and the pursuit of a genuinely fulfilling legal career.

Dr. Jessica Cole is the director of the Lawyers and Judges Program with the Mississippi State Bar. She is a licensed professional counselor and board certified telemental health provider with over 20 years of experience in behavioral health. Prior to starting with the Mississippi Bar, she provided outreach services for residential treatment facilities covering Mississippi and Louisiana. Formerly, she held the director of psychological health position under the direction of the US Department of Defense (DoD) for over 8 years. Her experiences in behavioral health encompass many areas including inpatient, partial, and outpatient treatment focusing on issues including depression, addiction, and traumatic brain injury. Nationally, she was president of the Integrated Care Interest group for the American Counseling Association and frequently provides lectures on a variety of behavioral health topics. Dr. Cole received her doctorate of professional counseling from Mississippi College, her masters degree in counseling from Louisiana State University, and her bachelors degree in psychology from the University of Mississippi.

About the Author

Sir James Gray Robinson, Esq. is a third-generation trial attorney who specialized in family law and civil litigation for 27 years in his native North Carolina. Burned out, Sir James quit in 2004 and has spent the following 20 years doing extensive research and innovative training to help others facing burnout and personal crises to heal. He has taught wellness, transformation, and mindfulness internationally to thousands of private clients, businesses, and associations. He is focused on helping lawyers, professionals, entrepreneurs, employers, and parents facing stress, anxiety, addiction, depression, exhaustion, and burnout.

Sir James is a highly respected speaker, writer, TV personality, mentor, consultant, mastermind, movie producer, and spiritual leader/healer who is committed to healing the planet. He possesses over 30 certifications and degrees in law, healing, and coaching, as well as hundreds of hours of post-certification training in the fields of neuroscience, neurobiology, and neuroplasticity, epigenetics, mind-body-spirit medicine, and brain/heart integration. Having experienced five near-death experiences has given him a deeper connection with divinity, understanding, and spiritual energy.

Sir James has written 13 books. In recognition of his outstanding work and philanthropy, Sir James was recently knighted by the Royal Order of Constantine the Great and Saint Helen. He recently received the 2024 International Impact Book Award and the Presidential Lifetime Achievement Award from President Joe Biden. You can learn more about his work and opportunities for transformation at: www.jamesgrayrobinson.com.

Introduction

In the legal profession, the pursuit of justice often comes at a cost—a toll on the mental health and well-being of lawyers. Burnout, depression, and elevated rates of anxiety are critical issues affecting the legal community. Recent studies from Massachusetts, California, and the District of Columbia reveal alarming statistics, shedding light on the mental health challenges within the profession.

I am not writing this book as an academic exercise. In 2004, at the height of my legal career, I had a nervous breakdown and quit practicing law. I was a third-generation trial lawyer in North Carolina, AV rated in the Martindale-Hubbell law directory by my peers. I had many friends and colleagues. Yet, despite doing everything "right," I was hiding a dark secret that nearly destroyed my soul. I was desperately unhappy, wrestling with demons, post-traumatic stress disorder (PTSD), and addiction.

I looked to alternative medical practices to heal myself. I had been in conventional "talk" therapy for years, but it wasn't even scratching the surface of the demons of my past, my obesity, my exhaustion, and my shame. I felt something new was required to heal my deep-seated issues, and I found it in alternative medicine and coaching.

I am writing this book to share a message of hope and redemption for all lawyers struggling with stress, anxiety, depression, and/or addiction. I have survived all those issues and want to guide you to the resilience you need to achieve happiness, satisfaction, confidence, and success. The identities of the lawyers that are discussed here have been changed to protect privacy, but the symptoms and the results are real.

One of the tragic byproducts of our suffering is the collateral damage that is inflicted on our families, friends, and clients due to our suffering. My pain and lack of ability to manage it cost me two marriages and hindered my relationship with my children and family. It wasn't until I found the way to heal that I could have a healthy, thriving romantic partnership.

It is possible to heal past wounds and relationships so that current relationships can thrive.

The Massachusetts study, conducted by Lawyers Concerned for Lawyers and the National Opinion Research Center at the University of Chicago, surveyed more than 4,000 attorneys, with disconcerting results. A staggering 77 percent reported feeling burned out, while 26 percent and 21 percent experienced high rates of anxiety and depression, respectively. More troubling was the revelation that 7 percent of respondents reported having suicidal thoughts—a figure higher than the national average among US adults. Additionally, a staggering 42 percent of lawyers disclosed engaging in unhealthy alcohol use.[1]

Notably, the COVID-19 pandemic, which was a backdrop to the survey, likely exacerbated stress levels and mental health challenges for lawyers. However, it truly amplified pre-existing concerns that lawyers face higher rates of mental health problems compared to the general population and other professions.

The California Lawyers Association and the District of Columbia Bar have unveiled groundbreaking research that highlights the personal and workplace factors that put lawyers at a heightened risk of suicidal thoughts. The study involved surveying 1962 individuals, of which approximately 8.5 percent reported experiencing thoughts of self-harm or feeling better off dead on a regular basis, indicating suicidal ideation. The research revealed that lawyers facing high work overcommitment were

2.2 times more likely to have suicidal thoughts, and those experiencing loneliness were 2.8 times more likely to endorse suicidality compared to their non-lonely counterparts.[2]

Gender also played a significant role, with men being twice as likely as women to report suicidal thoughts. Lawyers with a history of mental illness were 1.8 times more likely to endorse suicidality compared to those without such a history. Additionally, higher levels of perceived stress were associated with a higher likelihood of having suicidal thoughts, with lawyers experiencing high stress levels being 22 times more likely to report suicidal ideation compared to those with low perceived stress levels. Intermediate stress levels were associated with 5.5 times higher odds of endorsing suicidality.

These studies reveal an urgent need to address the well-being of lawyers. Structural changes, including reducing unrealistic time pressures and streamlining workloads, are crucial to alleviating stress in the profession. Additionally, creating supportive work environments with kindness, respect, and access to mentorship can positively impact lawyers' mental health. The practice of law does not need to be toxic to our mental and emotional health. If traditions are counterproductive, they must be changed. We need to expand our consciousness and make the practice of law more user friendly.

This book serves as a wake-up call to the legal profession, shedding light on the concerning rates of burnout, depression, anxiety, and suicidal thoughts among lawyers. By understanding the real causes, implementing strategies for a healthier work environment, cultivating resilience, seeking support, and advocating for change, we can transform the legal profession into a more compassionate, supportive, and mentally healthy community. Together, let us prioritize well-being and create a future where lawyers can thrive both personally and professionally.

1 Unmasking the Hidden Struggles: The State of Lawyer Well-Being

In the high-stakes world of law where justice is sought, battles are fought, and lives hang in the balance, a hidden adversary silently wages war on the legal profession—the state of lawyer well-being. Behind the prestigious titles and confident courtroom personas, lawyers grapple with myriad challenges that threaten their mental health and overall sense of fulfillment. In this unfiltered exploration, we shed light on the state of lawyer well-being, unmasking the hidden struggles that legal professionals across the nation face.

In the later stages of my 27-year active legal practice, I spent a lot of time on domestic family law cases. Divorces, custody battles, property division, and "heart balm actions" seemed to consume a lot of my time. These were made even more stressful to me because I had gone through the same issues personally during my two divorces. Psychologically, the potential loss of control of relationships, finances, and property come together in a perfect storm to bring out the worst behavior in people.

My experience was that these pressures turned lawyers into being less collegiate, more litigious, and more unreasonable. This change probably was caused by their clients who were going through what likely would prove to be the worst time of *their* lives. In my opinion, the judicial system is not designed to heal people's emotional wounds during divorce and custody battles. Clients' unfounded fears for their children often overwhelm their common sense and create an epic—and expensive—battle for control of the other parent.

I often had to explain to clients that their former spouse and co-parent was not the spawn of Satan, and that they cared for their children as much as they did themselves. This often fell on deaf ears. Trying to teach co-parenting skills to two people who could not communicate in a meaningful way about anything was even more stressful than guiding them through the legal process. It was difficult not to feel guilty when a client didn't get what they wanted.

It seemed at times that I was required to be a mental and emotional coach more than a lawyer to get my client through the process. It was often impossible for me to disassociate myself with my client's fears that they carried through the process. If a judge ruled against my client, even though it didn't happen very often, I sometimes took it personally. This fed into my imposter syndrome and perfectionist issues (discussed later) and made my life extremely uncomfortable.

I find that too often lawyers take it personally when their clients don't get what they want, especially when the client's "ex" does something hurtful. One of the most stressful aspects of being a family lawyer in emotionally charged cases is the fact that many judges tend to discount our client's fears and try to balance the conditions of custody and visitation. When the unthinkable happens, such as a child gets hurt or is kidnapped, it is difficult for lawyers not to privately feel responsible.

I remember when a client's child was kidnapped and taken overseas to a jurisdiction that did not respect US laws. We got them back through extrajudicial means, and throughout the process, I suffered as much as my client. This identification with the client is probably one of the reasons I burned out; I did not have the tools to separate myself from their pain.

1.1 THE BURNOUT EPIDEMIC: A LEGAL CRISIS

Within the legal profession, the term "burnout" has become more than a buzzword; it's an epidemic and a crisis that cannot be ignored. Lawyers experience the intense pressure of high-stakes cases, unrelenting deadlines, and an "always-on" culture. The consequences are undeniable: A decline into burnout relentlessly erodes their mental and emotional resilience.

According to the recent Massachusetts study, a staggering 77 percent of respondents reported feeling burned out. The relentless pursuit of justice leaves attorneys emotionally drained and mentally exhausted, chipping away at their passion for the law they once held dear. The study further revealed that 40 percent of lawyers had considered leaving the legal profession entirely within the past three years due to burnout and stress. This attrition rate poses a serious threat to the sustainability of the legal profession, leaving us to question how we can preserve the talent and dedication of our legal community.

To put these startling numbers into context, in 2016, the American Bar Association (ABA) and the Hazelton Betty Ford Foundation conducted a nationwide survey of approximately 13,000 lawyers and judges about their mental health, substance abuse, and well-being. The results were alarming.[3]

Approximately 36.4 percent qualified as problem drinkers. Not only were the statistics on substance abuse frightening (three times the national average), but 28 percent reported being depressed, 19 percent reported struggling with anxiety, and 23 percent experienced stress. All these statistics were much higher than national averages.[4]

It was this study that led me to focus on helping attorneys transform their stress into success. I had trained since 2004 to be skilled in mentoring professionals about the pressures and stress of their work and helping them heal. Given my long history in the law industry, I felt the need to concentrate on attorneys. Since then, I have helped lawyers across the country and other professionals overcome their problems with work, life, and substance abuse.

After the disturbing 2016 report was published, the ABA and state bar associations implemented programs to help lawyers. State supreme courts implemented continuing legal education (CLE) requirements for well-being and mental health. No one knew whether the programs that state bar associations implemented were having any effect, but in the interim, COVID-19 completely changed the way we practiced law. We had to work from home or over the internet. Even trials were conducted via Zoom calls.

I suspected that these radical changes would have a negative impact on attorney well-being, and the recent survey by the Massachusetts Bar Association proved me right. The numbers were substantially worse than they were reported in 2016. I will discuss why later, but it is obvious that what conventional therapy proposes is not working.

In the last two years, I have spoken to dozens of groups of attorneys, both privately and publicly, about causes of and solutions for stress, anxiety, substance abuse, and depression. I have spoken at ABA meetings; state bar meetings in California, Michigan, and North Carolina; at the Judicial Conference of the United States in New York; and at numerous local bar meetings. I have written dozens of articles that were published in legal journals across the nation, including the *ABA Journal*.[5]

For the reasons outlined earlier, I have a special place in my heart for attorneys who practice family law. As I indicated, the judicial process is not particularly healing for the parties that have to go through the courts to try to separate their lives and fortunes. Although there are no direct statistics that analyze the emotional and mental issues that family law attorneys experience compared to their colleagues, I suspect that family law attorneys are probably as stressed as, if not more than, lawyers in general. At least emotionally, it seems that more is at stake for the parties, their families, and their children.

1.2 ANXIETY AND DEPRESSION: UNINVITED COMPANIONS

The legal battleground is littered with casualties, and lawyers are not immune to the ravages of mental health challenges that follow in its wake. The stark reality revealed by the Massachusetts study is damning: 26 percent of respondents endure crippling anxiety while 21 percent bear the weight of depression. These numbers expose the hidden struggles that countless legal professionals face—far removed from the prying eyes of the public.

The immense pressure of legal responsibilities can leave lawyers gasping for air, drowning in a sea of overwhelming anxiety. The constant scrutiny, the insatiable demand for perfection, and the paralyzing fear of failure all conspire to brew a toxic cocktail of anxiety that lawyers are forced to imbibe daily. Shackled by the stigma surrounding mental health, they silently endure their emotional turmoil, their suffering unnoticed and unaddressed.

Depression, a stealthy intruder, prowls the halls of the legal profession. It lurks in the shadows undetected. Its insidious presence remains camouflaged beneath the veneer of professional success, concealed by the illusion of strength, resilience, and unwavering competence that lawyers project. Behind closed doors, however, depression takes hold, casting its suffocating shadow over even the most accomplished legal minds.

At times, my own struggle with depression was overwhelming. It felt like I was exhausted all the time, and my past was weighing me down to the point that I literally couldn't stand up straight. I was continuously worrying about what people were thinking about me and whether I was going to be disbarred for incompetence. I magnified every setback or adverse result into evidence of my incompetence.

The depression caused me to ignore all evidence of success that I was experiencing, as I turned small setbacks into major defeats in my mind. I found it hard to have a sense of humor, and I rarely smiled. I could make other people smile and laugh, but I could not feel joy or happiness. It felt like everyone was looking over my shoulder and secretly questioning every move I made. The fact that two of my partners were my father and my brother multiplied my feelings of isolation and pain.

Overly sensitive to any criticism or advice, no matter how kindly it was offered, I blundered through my days, always emotionally on edge. My secretary knew something was bothering me but knew better than to ask. All my inner resources were committed to my clients' well-being. I had nothing to give to myself. I quit exercising and ballooned to 250 pounds. Obesity set in. Someone who always enjoyed physical exercise and competition, I could hardly climb a flight of stairs.

Depression is defined as a mood disorder that causes a persistent feeling of sadness and loss of interest in life in ways that can interfere with daily functioning.[6] It can be temporary or long-term, low-key or intense. Both the symptoms and the causes can vary with great extremity, further complicating the cycle.

Research indicates that depression can be caused by chemical imbalances in the brain that might be genetically inherited or driven by stressful environments that trigger traumatic reactions in the brain. Other causes include illness and medical issues, substance abuse, and personality disorders.[7]

When lawyers start talking about stress (it is becoming a common topic), they are usually talking about the effect that their law practice has on their feeling of well-being, their self-value, and their self-esteem. In a recent ALM Mental Health Survey of the Legal Profession (2023), 38 percent of lawyers surveyed felt that they were depressed. This is four times the depression rate of the general population.[8]

What is alarming about these statistics is that they are not going down, even though every state bar association has programs to support depressed lawyers, and more and more resources have been thrown at the problem. Probably even more troubling is the reluctance of lawyers to admit that they have a problem; it is conceivable that the reality of depression in lawyers is even more dire than the surveys show.

There are several symptoms cited as indicating depression in lawyers:

- Absence of joy or happiness. Tasks that used to be exciting and fun feel like a burden or a hurdle.
- Pervasive negative emotions. Feelings of regret, remorse, guilt, fear, anger, worthlessness, and shame seem to dominate the internal landscape and are hard to self-correct.
- Focusing on the worst-case scenario becomes overwhelming and leads to negative overthinking. Rather than using our rational minds to discover what can go right, we totally obsess about what can go wrong.
- Substance overuse and abuse becomes a problem.
- Difficulty resting or getting quality sleep becomes insomnia. Conversely, oversleeping and sleeping too much can also become a problem.
- Health issues surface, causing fluctuations in weight and appetite, and chronic pain.
- Isolation, withdrawal, and listlessness impact personal and professional relationships.[9]

Lawyers often wonder why they are susceptible to depression. I have found that the truth is that the same set of factors that make individuals choose to become a lawyer can cause depression:[10]

- **Compassion.** For most, a lawyer chooses their profession for altruistic reasons (as well as to seek financial compensation and respect). They see problems in the world and want to do something about them, which is the true definition of compassion. Depression arises when they run head-on into the practice of law, which is highly competitive and critical to our nation's operation. All lawyers can do is the best they can based on their education and experience, which does not guarantee any outcomes. When we allow the disappointment of unachieved results to overwhelm us, we are subject to depression.
- **Perspective.** A universal truth is that what we perceive is what we want to see. In other words, we see the world through colored lenses that are installed by our life experiences. Our biases, beliefs, opinions, traumas, and tribes (friends and family) influence how we react to life's ups and downs. If those components do not support us in times of stress, we can easily crack under the strain of a law practice.
- **Excellence/perfectionism.** Lawyers are trained to be perfect, or at least more perfect than their opponent. Throughout their education and law school, excellence was rewarded. When we start practicing law, the results upon which we judge ourselves are often beyond our control. It doesn't matter how hard we work, sometimes we won't get what we want. This reality can be viewed as failure, which is unacceptable to many lawyers. Simply doing a great job is often not good enough.

- **Imposter syndrome.** This is a problem I see in many of my clients. Lawyers feel like they don't know what they are doing—primarily because of the complexities of the practice of law. Lawyers often believe that if their clients discover their "incompetence," they will be disbarred or fired. It doesn't matter how experienced or highly trained someone is; the uncertainty of practicing law can be overwhelming. Most have gone through law school with the expectation or hope that at some point they will feel competent and in control. However, the truth is that the uncertainty of the practice of law is fundamental to the profession, and until we can come to grips with that uncertainty, we are at risk of depression. This is true whether you are a trial lawyer, a criminal lawyer, a business lawyer, or an estate planner.
- **Post-traumatic stress disorder (PTSD).** This syndrome is applicable not only to first responders and military personnel, but to lawyers as well. Secondary PTSD is especially pervasive and happens not only to the lawyers, but also to their staff. Secondary PTSD occurs when caregivers are exposed to their client's' trauma over a long period of time. Without having proper wellness practices in place, it is inevitable that the caregiver can experience depression. Ironically, the more compassionate the lawyer is, the more at risk for secondary PTSD they are.

We must understand that depression is the psyche's way of protecting itself when there is a glitch in the software.[11] In other words, we are perceiving the practice of law in a flawed manner, and it can be corrected. A multitude of articles about self-care and well-being have been published.

In my experience, the practice of law is like a three-legged stool. To avoid the stress and depression that affects a substantial portion of lawyers, a lawyer needs (1) a sense of humor, (2) strategies for stress management and health, and (3) a supportive group of people surrounding them. Without any one of these, a lawyer is susceptible to burnout. When you experience symptoms of depression, it should be a flag that you need to bolster the foundation of your wellness.[12]

I have seen rapid improvement in levels of depression and stress when lawyers take heed of their symptomatology and take strategic action to change their mindset, health, and well-being. Our emotions, thoughts, and behaviors are all interconnected and must be observed. Otherwise, the symptoms of depression will intensify, and burnout will occur.

1.3 SUICIDAL THOUGHTS: A CRY FOR HELP

Let's face the cold, hard truth that 7 percent of lawyers grappled with suicidal thoughts per the bone-chilling revelations of the Massachusetts study. This gut-wrenching statistic is an unapologetic wake-up call, a jarring reminder that the legal community must confront the deep-rooted issues that fuel this distressing reality.

The incessant pressures of the legal profession, combined with feelings of isolation and vulnerability, push some lawyers perilously close to the edge of despair. We can't shy away from addressing the grim truths that lead lawyers to contemplate suicide. It's time to provide lawyers with the unwavering support and resources that they need to grasp hope and find a path to healing.[13]

It is ironic in the extreme that the character traits that make good lawyers can make them burnout. Lawyers care. That is why we make the sacrifices that are required to be successful and effective. We work long hours, we deal with adversity daily, and we often are criticized for what we do. We are compassionate in that we feel the pain of others, and we want to help.

Problems arise when lawyers regularly deal with traumatized clients in stressful situations. Without proper boundaries, lawyers often are overwhelmed by the trauma and stress of their clients. In medical terms, this is called compassion fatigue, and it is common among medical care professionals, first responders, and attorneys.[14]

Symptoms of compassion fatigue include emotional and physical exhaustion, anger, irritability, addiction to mood-enhancing substances, career dissatisfaction, and impaired judgment. It occurs when lawyers are repeatedly exposed to clients who are struggling with trauma or stress and when lawyers aren't properly trained to deal mentally and emotionally with these stressors over long periods of time. The cumulative effect of witnessing secondhand stress, anxiety, and depression eventually leads to the symptoms of those conditions appearing in the attorney.[15]

Medical experts differentiate between burnout and compassion fatigue. Although the symptoms are similar, compassion fatigue develops in a shorter time because of the intensity of the suffering. Not only do attorneys experience these symptoms, but their judgment also tends to be impaired, and they blame others for their suffering. They often engage in counterproductive behavior such as quitting, getting a divorce, having an affair, self-medicating, or ignoring their health. Burnout and compassion fatigue are, unfortunately, human responses to overwhelming tragedy and stress.

In the forthcoming chapters of this journey, we'll plumb the depths of the factors that impact lawyer well-being and the profound toll it takes on our profession. Through honest examination of these harsh realities, we empower ourselves to forge real change. We can become a legal community that values mental health above all else. Together, we'll unveil the path toward a healthier and more fulfilling legal profession, not just for ourselves, but for generations to come.

1.4 THE SOURCE OF STRESS

We all deal with stress, but where does it come from? Many times, life throws curve balls that we weren't expecting. Why do we experience stress or anxiety when something unexpected happens? Is it as simple as that when something happens that we don't like, we are stressed? Or is it just a symptom of fear of the future? Is there any way to eliminate stress from our lives?

Common sources of stress for lawyers include:[16]

- Overwork
- Multiple caseloads and deadlines
- Personality
- Physical and emotional health
- Relationships
- Change
- Financial problems
- Unexpected challenges
- The death of a loved one
- Substance abuse[17]

The starting point to eliminating stress is to realize that triggers to our stress may have been formed early in life. Perhaps your parents were struggling to make ends meet and were constantly sending negative messages to you about money. Messages of lack, bad luck, that life is unfair, and blame and anxiety about money create similar patterns in young, impressionable children.

Perhaps your parents struggled with their relationship. Messages of guilt, shame, jealousy, rejection, abandonment, or insecurity might easily have created triggers in the young minds of their children as they looked on. Often buried memories and feelings bubble up later in life as stress. If your parents often expressed feelings of victimhood, you will have learned how to react to life in similar ways. Our parents are oftentimes the source of our anxiety because that is how they taught us to experience life, and that anxiety is a necessary part of life.[18]

If we were programmed for perfection, we were set up for stress. I am not talking about the perfection of acceptance; I am talking about the concept that everything must happen as we plan it. Basically, we believe that if we don't get what we want, there is something wrong with us. As life is what happens when we had something else planned, a program of perfection in carrying out our plan will create stress. The more expectations that we have, the more anxiety and stress we will have. If we were always trying to be perfect little boys and girls to please our parents, trying to find the approval of others, trying to get the attention of parents or authority figures, stress was our constant invisible companion.

If our parents were highly judgmental and constantly criticized us or others, we also learned to be judgmental in our life view. By constantly perceiving that the world is wrong and you are right, the tension between wrong and right produces stress. In young children, observing negative talk often instills negative self-talk in the child. When all we do is constantly criticize ourselves, we create the feeling of anxiety through self-hatred.[19]

Many lawyers suffer from low self-esteem, and this contributes to their stress. They are presented with numerous opportunities to be self-critical and beat themselves up. Lawyers and others who suffered childhood abuse or trauma are more likely to suffer from low self-esteem.[20]

1.5 OVERWHELM

Many times, I felt overwhelmed by my circumstances, drowning in the thoughts and emotions related to my problems to the point of paralysis. Physically, I felt like I couldn't breathe and was enveloped in a dense brain fog.

A sense of overwhelming occurs when the intensity of our emotions overcomes our ability to manage them. Seemingly small events cause us to spin out of control, and we overreact. We lose our ability to think clearly and deal with the normal pressures of any given day. Many of my clients feel this way when they come to me. They are at their wit's end and don't know what to do.

As we shall see, dealing with being overwhelmed is simple. You don't have to panic or quit. If I had known the information and skills that I learned and have set out below, I probably would still be actively practicing law and enjoying it. Read on, dear friends, and discover a totally new approach to overcoming life's challenges.[21]

2 The Legal Profession's Silent Sufferers: Unraveling the Mental Health Crisis

Behind the polished veneer of legal brilliance and unwavering professionalism lies a dark reality that society often overlooks—the silent suffering of lawyers grappling with mental health challenges. In this chapter, we peel back the layers and expose the raw truth of the mental health crisis within the legal profession. We dive deep, unearthing the contributing factors that perpetuate this crisis and shedding light on the dire consequences of neglecting mental well-being. It's time to confront the uncomfortable truths that have been hidden from public view for far too long.

2.1 THE HIGH-PRESSURE ENVIRONMENT: AN INCUBATOR FOR MENTAL STRUGGLES

The legal profession's high-pressure environment breeds mental health struggles with ruthless efficiency. Lawyers are thrust into a pressure cooker, where vulnerability is shunned and self-care is deemed a luxury for the weak. Lawyers' quest for excellence becomes an all-consuming mandate, leaving little time to process the whirlwind of emotions and experiences that assail them.[22]

Law schools are structured to train otherwise highly intelligent people to think in a very particular way—extremely logically and to analyze real-world problems in a legal context. In other words, mind control.[23] I can remember the first lecture I attended in law school. The professor asked if there were any poets in the room. I was the only one who raised my hand. I was an English major in college and relished writing poetry. The professor looked straight at me and said, "We will train that out of you." What I didn't realize was, he was talking about training me to think like lawyers are supposed to think. Any time an institution starts interfering with how people think, there will be casualties. I was one.

When lawyers analyze problems (legal issues), they are trained to think in terms of the past. We are trained to see how problems were decided in the past, regardless of whether the decision was effective or practical. A saying I heard many times about jurisprudence is "creativity" and "outside-the-box thinking" is discouraged. Everything must be filtered through the lens of **stare decisis**, which means that "we have always done it that way," and this is how problems will be solved in the future. For many lawyers with creative and inspired thinking, this is like putting a square peg in a round hole.[24]

2.2 THE PERFECTIONIST'S DILEMMA: STRIVING FOR THE UNATTAINABLE

Lawyers are often driven by a pursuit of perfection—a double-edged sword that can have devastating consequences on their mental well-being. The quest to achieve the unattainable becomes a breeding ground for anxiety and self-doubt, a constant state of unease that gnaws at their very core.[25]

The very things that make great lawyers may also make them miserable. Growing up, we were overachievers, seeking extra credit, going the extra mile, doing whatever needed to be done to get the highest grades. Achievement equaled value. If we did not get more than 100 (of course many of us went for the extra credit) on a test, we failed. This is the curse of perfectionism, the quest for excellence metastasized into an obsession with results.

Countless lawyers have crashed and burned because they couldn't be the best. Their psyches couldn't handle not billing the most hours, not winning every case, constantly raising the bar of what they considered success. Their opinion of themselves is generally based entirely on their level of productivity. Typically, workaholics ignore their health to get the result that proves their value. They tell themselves that if they work hard and sacrifice, then one day they will be happy. That day never comes.

We have replaced our angel godmother with an autocratic nun with a ruler. Our psyches have stopped being positive and creative and started being negative and critical. We are obsessed with control in a profession that doesn't deal in absolutes. It is not enough to provide excellent legal representation; our clients want results. At times, these results can challenge our integrity and ethical obligations. Yet the ends justify the means if our reputations are enhanced.

The problem lies in the fact that we externalize our sense of self and have become uber codependent. We are people pleasers and have totally disempowered ourselves to others.[26] We live according to other people's standards, not our own. Fear of failure dictates our work ethic, not the sense of accomplishment of a job well done. Lawyers live in a world where a single typo in a 200-page document proves that they are incompetent. We can overreact over insignificant details and self-destruct when anything adverse happens. It may truly be a detail that is a needle in a haystack, yet these micro mistakes can be made paramount in our minds.

The obsessive concern of what other people think differentiates perfectionistic lawyers from their peers who are emotionally and mentally healthy. A saying among mental health professionals is, "What other people think of me is none of my business." A perfectionistic lawyer's saying is, "What other people think of me is my only business."[27]

This perfectionistic thinking causes suffering: anxiety, rigidity, closed-mindedness, defensiveness, lack of trust (isolationism), blame, and shame. I remember representing a client in an appellate argument before the Fourth Circuit Court of Appeals. Opposing counsel was competent and seemingly confident. It was clear during the hearing that my client would win. Immediately after the hearing, the opposing counsel went into the restroom and vomited for 20 minutes. I could relate.

Lawyers are supposed to conduct due diligence, analyze what could go wrong, and help their clients avoid any risks that are involved. I call this "worst-case scenario thinking." We have put ourselves in the position of claiming power over the future and control over things we can't control. Even worse, we apply this mode of thinking to our personal lives and to the people we love and appear autocratic and unfeeling. We appear to "know it all" and lack flexibility.

Another cause of stress is a condition known as "imposter syndrome." This is an internal belief that's both conscious and unconscious that a lawyer is a fraud or a "phony" who will eventually be discovered, drawn, and quartered.[28] This is true even when external evidence proves contrary, as the lawyer may excel in external, objective ways. I was the poster child for this condition.

Every waking moment was underscored with the panic that someone would find out that I didn't know as much as I should, that I was flying by the seat of my pants, or that my successes were more attributable to luck or chance than to skill and preparation. At least 50 percent of my thoughts were analyzing how to hide my fears, my mistakes, and my self-contempt.

The focus of my obsessive thinking was not on how to win and succeed, it was on how to avoid losing and to not fail. The difference between the two was years of stress, anxiety, and shame. Any result that was less than 100 percent of what I wanted was evidence that I was incompetent. For mentally and emotionally healthy attorneys, achieving 90 percent of the intended results was acceptable. For me, it was not.

I was an expert at worst-case scenario thinking. All lawyers analyze what could go wrong or anticipate opposing arguments to better represent their clients. My problem was I was applying this analysis to everything, from what I would say to someone if they criticized me to how I would respond to family and friends. There was a constant Greek chorus in my mind chanting "woe."

The biggest problem with worst-case scenario thinking is we are never fully present in the moment. We don't listen because we are always thinking of the response rather than hearing what the other person has to say. We are so focused on not being wrong that we rarely hear or comprehend what is being said. We must be right, because if we admit we're wrong, it constitutes evidence that we are a failure or a fraud. I could not allow myself to be open-minded or flexible.[29]

This doomsday mental state is focused on how things will go wrong instead of things that will go right. We are overwhelmed with the "problems" and can only see the downside. This guarantees that we will stay in worst-case scenario mode looking for mistakes and miss the potentials and opportunities. We start obsessing on not being wrong rather than on being right. This constant thought pattern creates neural pathways in our brain that cause us to constantly obsess on the problems rather than look for solutions. When we create those neural pathways, we manifest our worst fears and prove we are failures.[30]

Beneath the surface lies a profession built on scrutiny and critique, where every word, every decision, every action is subject to the merciless judgment of peers, clients, and superiors. The fear of falling short, of facing disapproval, amplifies the suffocating pressure to be flawless. This unrelenting pursuit of perfection can lead to a downward spiral of mental struggles as lawyers find themselves trapped in a cycle of self-criticism and unattainable expectations.

I can remember when I graduated near the top of my class at Wake Forest University School of Law in 1978 and was hired by one of the premier law firms in the Southeast. It was no coincidence that my father was one of the senior partners. I was fulfilling his dream for me, to follow in his footsteps.

Despite all the training I received in law school, I was ill-prepared for the pressures of practice in a large law firm. Minimum billable hours (40 hours/week) and navigating the unfamiliar territory of the courtroom with real consequences for mistakes amplified the pressure to succeed. I felt I was under a microscope, especially from the partners who wanted an anti-nepotism clause in the partner agreement.

I began developing a deeply rooted imposter syndrome, which many lawyers struggle with—the feeling that if my colleagues and clients discovered how scared and inexperienced I was, I would be fired on the spot. Even decades later, that feeling followed me until it blossomed into my nervous breakdown. It didn't matter how many cases I won or the millions of dollars in fees I generated. I never escaped the fear of discovery of my incompetence.

I was living in conflict, the joy of a successful practice battling the fear of discovery. I magnified the small mistakes that occur in every law practice into perceived gross errors in judgment. I was terrified that I would receive a letter from the ethics committee of the state bar any day. My family had no clue I was so conflicted. They just knew I wasn't happy. Just as many lawyers are likely to do, I suppressed my insecurities and never sought help for my declining mental health.[31]

2.3 THE SILENT STIGMA: MENTAL HEALTH TABOOS IN THE LEGAL WORLD

In the legal world, where high stress, relentless work, and high-stakes responsibilities are the norm, mental health concerns often remain shrouded in silence. The legal profession's relentless demands have contributed to a culture where discussing mental health issues is often seen as a sign of weakness or incompetence. This silent stigma surrounding mental health poses significant barriers to seeking help and support, hindering the overall well-being of legal professionals.

If there is one common denominator of the many attorneys and paralegals I have helped, it is the fear of the stigma, that if they reach out for help, people will think there is something fundamentally wrong with them.[32]

While I was an attorney in North Carolina, I served on the Lawyers Assisting Lawyers (LAL) committee. I earned my way onto this committee after being arrested for driving under the influence twice. I went through in-patient rehabilitation, which I was released from early, as even in rehab I was committed to being an overachiever. I stayed sober for one year, which was the minimum period of sobriety to serve on the LAL committee.

My role with the LAL committee was to intervene with lawyers who had been reported to the North Carolina State Bar for being drunk in court or with clients. I had the reputation of being a hatchet man because I basically delivered the message that the lawyer had to submit to rehabilitation or face a grievance procedure. If they submitted to rehabilitation, the matter would remain confidential and not be public.

If they refused to go to rehabilitation, a grievance would be filed with the state bar, and the attorney would have to go through a public grievance process. (This was only available if the lawyer had not violated any other ethics rules.) This may sound harsh, but it was a lifeline that the state bar offered to an attorney with substance abuse problems. Only two lawyers I met with refused to go to treatment. I was saddened to hear that both eventually died from substance abuse complications.

Lawyers are exceptionally clever. One of the lawyers on whom I had to do an intervention insisted that she did not have a "drinking problem," despite court personnel complaining that she smelled of alcohol during court proceedings. She was glassy-eyed and had trouble speaking when I met with her about the complaints. She continued to deny "drinking" and insisted that the court personnel were wrong.

She agreed to go to rehabilitation after I explained to her that if she didn't go, a grievance would be filed against her, and the accusations would be made public. I later found out that she was, in fact, not "drinking" alcohol. She was going to the length of soaking food in vodka and eating the food. Fortunately, rehabilitation was effective, and she took control of her life again, becoming a much better attorney.

The problem with simply stopping the abuse of substances or drugs is that it doesn't heal the causes of the substance abuse. The saying goes that "If you sober up a horse thief, you still have a horse thief." Whatever negative emotions, thoughts, or beliefs that drive people to self-medicate will still be present if unaddressed. This makes it highly likely that the attorney will return to self-medication or become addicted to something else to attempt to alleviate the problems.

This is why 12-step programs aren't effective for at least 50 percent of the people who enter them. There is no trained inquiry of the real cause of the addiction, whether it is adverse childhood experiences, anxiety, depression, or mental or emotional disorders. It is critical to uncover the cracks in the foundation that lead to self-medication. Without healing the foundation, sobriety is like a house of cards that can crumble under the weight of adversity or stress.[33]

A. The Fear of Perceived Weakness

In the competitive and demanding legal world, individuals often feel pressured to project an image of strength and invulnerability. This fear of being perceived as weak or incapable can deter lawyers from acknowledging their struggles with mental health. The stigma surrounding mental health further compounds this issue, leading to a reluctance to seek help and perpetuating a harmful cycle where issues remain unaddressed and worsen over time.

One major reason for this stigma is the perception that seeking help for mental health challenges is a sign of weakness. Lawyers are often expected to be tough, resilient, and capable of handling any challenge that comes their way. Admitting to mental health struggles may be viewed as a sign of inadequacy, causing many legal professionals to suffer in silence rather than seek the support they need.[34]

If there is one common denominator of the many attorneys and paralegals I have helped, it is the fear of the stigma that people will think there is something fundamentally wrong with us.

Most lawyers are afraid that if they sought help, then "someone would find out," and they would be stigmatized. Unfortunately, this prevents them from reaching out for help before they get into legal trouble or have ethical problems. I was one of these unfortunates that knew there were resources available, but I didn't want to deal with disclosure. I chose "white knuckling" the problem rather than seeking help. I didn't access resources until I was faced with jail time.

This is one of the biggest objections I hear when I speak to lawyers about investing in my programs to eliminate stress, anxiety, and addiction. Potential clients are scared to death that my files will be hacked, or I would be subpoenaed in an action against them. I always assure them that it would be highly likely that I wouldn't remember any details of our conversations without notes, and I don't keep records of our conversations.

More importantly, I stress that the risk of getting better is far smaller than the risk of not doing anything. It only takes six hours with me to get relief from a lifetime of struggle. I ask clients to weigh the cost of a lifetime of struggle against the value of healing. If they don't get help, people will eventually notice their pain and suffering. If they heal, people will notice how much better they feel and behave. It can be a simple decision as to which choice they make.

A case in point is "Jamie," a lawyer from North Carolina who was having trouble with binge drinking. He had just started his own law firm after leaving a large law firm in a major metropolitan area. He was a transactional business lawyer who had found a lucrative niche in startup technology companies. He had just hired associates and was feeling the weight of the world on his shoulders.

Jamie had heard me speak at a local bar association meeting and called to ask me for advice about his drinking. He reported that he didn't drink every day, but normally on Friday, Saturday, and Sunday nights. He was getting concerned because he was experiencing blackouts, which were affecting his marriage. He wanted help managing his drinking.

It didn't take long to establish that he was struggling with imposter syndrome and perfectionism and didn't know how to turn off his highly critical mind. Even though there had not yet been evidence of negative behavior, he was overwhelmed with "what if's" and obsessive worst-case scenario thinking.

Jamie was a classic example of how quickly people can shift their reality when they are granted awareness of why they were thinking and feeling negatively and how to change their thoughts. We quickly sorted out the real cause of his fears and, with the techniques I use in my program, he was able to completely shift how he thought about his future. He no longer feared what might happen and got excited about what he was going to accomplish with his practice.

A few weeks after working with him, he reported that his drinking was under control, and his relationship with his wife was improving quickly. Even better, he enjoyed going to work and was interviewing for another associate.

B. The "Always-On" Culture

The legal profession's relentless "always-on" culture, defined by grueling working hours, unyielding deadlines, and constant connectivity, leaves scant space for rest and recuperation. In the pursuit of professional success, legal professionals may inadvertently neglect their mental and emotional well-being, sacrificing personal time and self-care.

This ingrained "burnout culture" not only takes a toll on their mental health but also perpetuates the stigma surrounding mental struggles. Admitting that one may be facing challenges becomes a daunting task due to the prevailing culture, making it difficult for individuals to seek the support they truly need.

Attorneys are highly familiar with the conflict between their law practice and their personal life. Culturally, we are currently calling it "work-life balance." The problem is, depending on the circumstances, there is no work-life balance when clients demand attention and tasks need to be done. When I went to law school in the 1970s, we learned from the first day of class that "the law is a jealous mistress."[35]

The meaning of that saying was lost on me until I became a partner in a small law firm. When I first started working at my father's firm, associates were expected to bill 40 hours or more a week. To come up with 40 billable hours, I was forced to work at least 80 hours per week.

When I became a partner in my own small law firm, I discovered that to pay the overhead and have a decent income, I needed to bill much more than 40 hours. This required me to be at work over 100 hours a week. We were responsible for bringing in revenues, no matter how long it took to achieve.

When I became a partner, that pressure to produce billable hours increased dramatically. We were responsible for bringing in revenues to pay for staff, associates, overhead, and operating costs. All of that came before what I got as a partner draw. Working long hours was no longer a choice.

There was something of a hero's journey involved, where I sacrificed my personal life for the good of the firm and my clients. I thought all my hard work would make my family proud, but it had the opposite effect. This work ethic was directly responsible for my two divorces. Neither of my wives could understand why I was working so hard late into the night. They suspected something else was going on.

There also is the self-defeating myth of "short-term pain for long-term gain." As lawyers, we are trained to believe that long hours and hard work to build a law practice in the beginning will pay off with larger revenues in the long run.[36] We should never sacrifice our health, family relationships, life outside of work, friends, or our integrity.

Thinking that making those sacrifices because we will be "rich" is a myth because, psychologically, there never is a payoff in the end. Many lawyers, especially the ones that burn out, keep working for more and more money. Their desire for this continuous increase in revenue becomes their sole reason for working.

Some of us bought into the archetypal sacrifice of the hero, the protagonist who offers his or her dreams on the altar of self-sacrifice in the service of others, to answer the challenge, to complete the quest, and establish a better world.[37] Unfortunately, the longer we stay on this sacrificial journey, the more ingrained that world becomes in our psyche, and neuroplasticity makes the sacrifice "normal."[38]

When I was a child, my father worked constantly. My mother insisted that he be home by supper, no later than 6 p.m. As he began to be more and more successful, he began to bring work home. He worked at night and on the weekends. My parents preached the virtues of sacrifice and that sacrifice made a "good" person. Conversely, appreciating yourself, accepting yourself, and desiring things for yourself was selfish. This was a common adage and myth of baby boomers—sacrifice now for pleasure later.

The problem for most attorneys, and especially for me, was that working long hours never stopped. I was always looking for the next client, the next fee, the next win. I assumed that my family was on board with this philosophy, but I was terribly wrong. They did not want an absentee husband and father.

I not only worked hard to make more money, but I was also trying to impress my father and brother. I felt like if I left the office after they did, that meant something. I felt like if I was the last man standing every night, night after night, it would impress them. The truth is that they didn't even notice. It was just me against myself, and each day I was losing ground.

C. Fear of Professional Consequences

Another factor contributing to the silence surrounding mental health is the fear of professional consequences. Lawyers may grapple with worries that opening up about their mental health challenges could tarnish their career prospects, damage their hard-earned reputations, or even trigger disciplinary actions. This pervasive fear acts as a formidable barrier, preventing individuals from reaching out for the help and support they desperately need. Consequently, the cycle of silence and isolation persists, hindering progress toward a more compassionate and supportive legal profession.

When I was at my lowest point, I was seeing danger behind every door and focusing on what could go wrong, instead of looking for what could go right. Even the most routine tasks became high-anxiety exercises in potential malpractice. When I was meeting with clients, instead of focusing on what they were saying, all I could think about was not screwing it up.

In my role as a counselor for the North Carolina State Bar Lawyers Assisting Lawyers program, I communicated regularly with the ethics committee. They rightly wanted to know the status of the various lawyers I was counseling. Every time I got a phone call from members of the ethics committee, a part of me would cringe because I was afraid that they were calling to accuse me of malpractice.

Instead of focusing on how I was helping and the positive results I was getting with the lawyers under my care, all I could think about was the guilt and shame of some future mistake. Even worse, I was terrified that I would violate some ethical rule that I didn't even know existed. My overactive ego was my own worst enemy.

I started spending more and more time by myself. I withdrew into my own little world and would keep the door to my office shut most of the time so I didn't have to deal with chit-chat or social conversations. My paranoia was slowly increasing. I imagined that my partners were furtively looking at me, knowing that I was incompetent but allowing me to practice only because my father was the senior partner.

I was winning awards for pro bono work, but the trophies I received were hidden in a hall closet. The partners didn't think pro bono work was commendable. I assumed they were rejecting me because they knew I was incompetent, despite evidence to the contrary. I was going through my second divorce, in my mind, further evidence of my incompetence. I was constantly asking myself, "How could they like me?"

Years later, after I quit, I came to understand that all that guilt and shame was a figment of my imagination. Former colleagues have told me that they had no such suspicions or ill will. They were genuinely concerned for my mental and emotional health. They didn't know what to do about it and assumed I was seeking help on my own. All of my suffering was self-inflicted, but I didn't ask for help because it would mean that my worst fears were correct.

D. The "Suck It Up" Culture

The legal profession has long been associated with a "suck it up" culture, where long hours, high stress, and self-sacrifice are normalized and even glorified. This culture may discourage lawyers from discussing their mental health openly, as it contradicts the traditional expectation of constant dedication and resilience. The pressure to conform to this culture can exacerbate mental health challenges and discourage individuals from seeking help.[39]

It took me several years after I quit to realize that my "suck it up" attitude was counterproductive. I often felt pride in my high threshold of pain and fortitude. Working long hours for decades had taken its toll on my mind and body, but my motto was straight out of the movie "*The Outlaw Josie Wales*": "Endeavor to persevere." It didn't occur to me that my over-the-top hard work ethic was killing me.

The problem was not only physical, but also mental and emotional. The constant exhaustion I was feeling and lack of balance in my life turned me into a surly, unhappy person.

I was angry, resentful, and mean. The consequences of ignoring a work–life balance were all too real for me.

What I didn't realize until years later was that it was a never-ending cycle of negative thought, emotion, and behavior. My negative thinking created negative beliefs, which created negative emotions, which created negative behavior. I thought I was doing what I was supposed to be doing. I was slowly imploding.

I see too many lawyers with this same symptomology of too much anxiety, fear, and depression. One of the worst cases I worked with was a lawyer named Juan in Los Angeles. He was a young partner in a mid-sized law firm and concentrated on domestic law. He complained of frequent headaches, binge drinking, and feeling depressed. It was obvious that he was fighting not only for his clients and against the opposition, but he was fighting his inner demons as well.

He had a thriving practice that was keeping him away from his family and any personal life. He was born into a poor household and his parents were immigrants from Central America. His father had died when he was young, and his mother had depended on him to help her raise his brothers and sisters. He felt a great deal of responsibility not only for his wife and children, but for his mother and siblings as well.

When I asked him when he felt happy, he said, "I don't have time to be happy! I have too many people depending on me." It took some time for him to change his mind set to being able to ask for help. It was a revelation to him that he was going down the same path that killed his father. He was willing to do whatever was necessary to avoid making his children feel the same way he had when his father died.

It was amazing how quickly his personal life and career changed when he started asking for help from his partners and his family. They were truly grateful to have him open and share what was going on with him. Both his partners and his family thought that he was angry with them without cause. When they found out he was struggling with not wanting to let anyone down, they quickly came up with solutions to let Juan have more time with his family.

When Juan was able to turn off his Warrior mode, he became a much more effective lawyer and a more loving father and husband. He started having fun at work and at home. His support staff were grateful that their boss was not so depressed and was easier to please. In other words, all of Juan's relationships improved and were more supportive.

E. Fear of Perceived Judgment

Lawyers, like any other professionals, may fear being judged or stigmatized by their peers and colleagues if they open up about their mental health struggles. The fear of being seen as incapable or unreliable can create a significant barrier, deterring individuals from opening up about their challenges. Consequently, this fear hinders the crucial opportunity for receiving much-needed support and understanding, perpetuating a culture of silence and isolation around mental health issues.[40]

I struggled with asking for help for most of my life. It always seemed to me that people who needed help were often marginalized by their colleagues and made to feel inferior. I had an inferiority complex that was overwhelming, and the thought of being perceived as weak or weak minded was unacceptable. As a result, my insecurity complex prevented me from asking for help.

I practiced law with my father and my brother and growing up my brothers and I competed for everything; bragging rights, test scores, our parents' love, and/or favoritism. We were encouraged to figure things out for ourselves. If I was unhappy, it was my responsibility and asking for help was a sign of laziness or stupidity.

The fear of disclosure included the fear of admitting that there was something wrong with me. This fed right into my imposter syndrome, my fear that if people really knew me, they wouldn't like me. Even worse, if I asked for help, it would be an admission that I wasn't good enough and/or incompetent. This fear kept me constantly stressed, anxious, and depressed.

Many people believe that those who suffer from burnout are somehow weak-minded or lost. I was cruelly criticized when I quit my law practice due to nervous exhaustion in 2004. Later I heard that I hid my pain so well that many people did not realize I was suffering. I think that is a common condition, we deny that we are suffering until we simply can't take it anymore.

Eventually, I did seek counseling from a psychotherapist. Not only was talk therapy not helpful, talking about the reasons that I was stressed, anxious and depressed made it worse. Once a week I had to remember all the mistakes, errors in judgment, shame, and guilt I had felt over the years. The therapist attempted to normalize my feelings by saying, "You should feel that way. If you didn't, I would be worried that you were a psychopath."

The psychotherapist completely missed the point that I was suffering from secondary trauma disorder. This is a problem for many attorneys who do personal injury, domestic, or divorce work. The pain and suffering of their clients is internalized by the lawyer because the lawyer cares. The lawyer cares about what happens to their client; that is why they are a lawyer. Compassion is a double-edged sword when the lawyer lets the pain felt by their client invade their psyche.[41]

Many of my clients practice domestic law. It is not surprising that their divorce and custody clients are experiencing all sorts of emotional pain and suffering. It doesn't matter if the lawyer is objective or strong willed, the constant exposure to their clients' fears will eventually cause the lawyer to suffer if the lawyer doesn't know how to handle it.

A perfect example of this was a client I had named Cathy who practiced domestic law. Cathy was in her 50s and a partner in a law firm in southern California. She had been a domestic/divorce attorney for decades, specializing in high value property divisions. I was originally contacted by one of her partners, who was concerned for Cathy's mental and emotional health.

Cathy was experiencing multiple physical symptoms of an overactive cortisol cycle. She was morbidly obese, taking stress medication, and was starting to have trouble making deadlines. She had blown up at her staff on several occasions, which had started causing her partners to be concerned about her mental health.

Cathy had several cases in the recent past that did not have the results her client wanted. Cathy had explained to the client from the outset about the uncertain nature of litigation and that many factors were beyond their control. To her credit, Cathy had accurately predicted some of the rulings that went against her client, but the client blamed her for the results.

It did not take long to identify that Cathy had been suffering from an overactive cortisol/adrenaline cycle which was causing insomnia, overeating, self-medicating, and depression. I was successful in training her how to use several techniques to relax, and I coached her into a better mindset. In a short period of time, Cathy was able to relax and enjoy her practice.

The most effective change for Cathy was the understanding that 95 percent of her fear and anxiety was between her ears. When she learned that she was projecting her fears onto her clients and staff, she could change that reality. She stopped blaming herself for things that were completely beyond her control and started problem solving the things she could control. Cathy's demeanor and behavior swiftly and completely changed.

F. Lack of Education and Awareness

Limited education and awareness about mental health issues within the legal community can contribute to the silence surrounding the topic. Without adequate understanding of mental health challenges and their impact, individuals may struggle to recognize their own struggles or support their colleagues effectively.

When I was a counselor for the NC State Bar Lawyers Assisting Lawyers committee, we all recognized that practicing law was a stressful profession. However, no one knew what was causing the stress or why lawyers were self-medicating. The only solution we had was intervention and rehabilitation.

The 2016 study was a call to arms for the American Bar Association (ABA) and the various state bar associations. CLE programs were prepared, and lawyers were ordered by their respective state supreme courts to attend these classes. The intention was to alert attorneys of the problem and to contact their state bar if they had a problem. This was problematic in two respects: (1) it didn't deal with the stigma lawyers associated with admitting they were struggling, and (2) the only solution was referral to talk therapists who weren't overly effective.

We were not prepared for the impact COVID-19 would have on the practice of law. The isolation and separation resulting from quarantining lawyers was devastating. No one knew the impact home practice and zoom calls would have on the psyche. The 2022 survey done by the Massachusetts Bar Association told the tale—the statistics had gotten much worse.

The stark reality revealed by the Massachusetts study cannot be ignored—26 percent of respondents endure crippling anxiety while 21 percent bear the weight of depression. All the work the ABA and state bars had done to help these issues were for naught. It seemed that COVID-19 had not only taken its toll on lawyers' health, but it had also severely damaged their resilience as well.

2.4 THE ISOLATED PRACTITIONER: LONELINESS IN THE LEGAL LANDSCAPE

In the world of law, there's a hidden truth that we must confront. While lawyers often work in teams and collaborate with colleagues, the nature of the profession can be inherently isolating. Beneath the surface of camaraderie, many legal professionals bear the weight of their work in solitude, struggling with feelings of disconnect and loneliness, fueling the fires of mental health struggles that rage within.[42]

The California and District of Columbia study found that lawyers with high work overcommitment and those who reported being lonely were significantly more likely to have suicidal thoughts. This correlation highlights the detrimental impact of isolation on the mental well-being of legal professionals.

I have helped several single practitioners who struggled with isolation. A good example was Don, an attorney who practiced in Pennsylvania. He had a successful practice, but his marriage was falling apart and he was having panic attacks. He felt marginalized because he wasn't feeling supported, and he felt alone. He was also mentoring several other single practitioners but was feeling negative emotions about his qualifications for guiding others.

COVID-19 only made matters much worse. Don rarely left his house; he conducted all his practice from there. He was considering giving up the lease on his office where he had practiced for decades because his income had decreased, and he wasn't using it anyway.

Don was experiencing migraines as well as chronic pain in his lower back. He was considering divorce and, because of COVID-19, had little or no support from family and friends. He didn't even contemplate asking for help. As a baby boomer, he held all the prejudices and biases that his generation grew up with. He wanted to be the strong, silent type. As a mentor, he believed that he couldn't afford to be perceived as weak.

Don was constantly stressed because of the changes to his practice and his failing marriage. He simply didn't know what to do. After our first session, I could tell that his demeanor had changed, and he had a completely different outlook on the future. By explaining to him the way his body was dealing with stress, he understood that he wasn't doing anything wrong. In fact, his body was doing what it was designed to do: protect him.

By teaching him some simple techniques to manage the stress and shift his perceptions, Don quickly began to see the opportunities in his situation, including having a relationship-changing conversation with his wife. When he opened up to her, the relationship healed in ways he couldn't have imagined. He contacted other colleagues and formed a mastermind group to brainstorm ways they could solve the problems COVID-19 had caused. His passion for the law was reignited as he aligned with his mission and his purpose a newfound wisdom of how to maintain balance, both internally and externally.

2.5 THE CALL FOR CHANGE: EMBRACING MENTAL HEALTH AS A PRIORITY

The mental health crisis in the legal profession demands action. It is time to break the silence surrounding mental health, challenge the stigma, and prioritize the well-being of lawyers. It's time to cut through the noise and prioritize mental health, no excuses.

We need a seismic shift that embraces openness, vulnerability, and genuine support. Mental health must become the bedrock of our profession, the cornerstone of our collective well-being.

The upcoming chapters will be our arsenal, armed with strategies to infuse a culture of mental well-being into the very fabric of the legal world. We can no longer turn a blind eye. We need to confront the challenges head-on, deploying proactive measures to empower lawyers to seize control of their mental health, igniting a flame that fuels their growth both professionally and personally.

Our minds are not always our friends. Our experience of life is largely based on what we believe. Implicit bias is a relatively recent concept in psychology/psychiatry which attempts to describe the unconscious prejudices and stereotypes which we form without conscious awareness. It is human nature to have biases, whether we want to admit to them or not.

Biases are formed through our education and experience, as well as our culture and history. It is generally recognized that our minds develop biases based on unconscious associations over time. Ironically, intelligence has nothing to do with it. In fact, the more intelligent one is, the higher the likelihood that you have implicit bias.[43]

Various studies have identified implicit bias in the legal world as it relates to: (1) hiring, promotion, pay, and responsibilities as these concepts are affected by gender, race, appearance, age, and sexual preferences; (2) jury selection; (3) client representation; and (4) relationships. Science explains that our minds are like icebergs, with our conscious awareness represented by the tip of the iceberg above the surface of the water, and our unconscious represented by the bulk iceberg below the surface of the water. We are not aware of the part of our mind which is unconscious (by definition).[44]

There is a test available online known as the Implicit Association Test (IAT) which was developed by psychologist Tony Greenwald and has torn the cover off implicit bias. It demonstrates that our concepts of "good/bad," "right/wrong," and "like/dislike" are the result of implicit bias, and no one is free from bias.[45]

As we become more and more familiar with the fact that a large part of our minds is unknown to us, we become more aware of the effects of our unconscious on our conscious minds. More specifically, when the conscious mind conflicts with our unconscious mind, the higher the chances are that we have anxiety, stress, and ultimately, burnout.[46]

In coaching attorneys who are experiencing burnout, stress, anxiety, or depression, I often find that there are unconscious traumas, beliefs, decisions, emotions, or thoughts that conflict with their goals, work, expectations, and dreams. Will power and determination only makes the conflict worse.

Like struggling in quicksand, white knuckles and clenched jaws only serve to make the struggle with hidden blocks more intense and lethal. Attorneys describe the effect metaphorically as like driving a car with one foot fully on the gas pedal and the other fully on the brake pedal. They feel like their wheels are spinning and yet they are not going anywhere. They feel stuck.

The new neuroscience behind implicit bias confirms that the unconscious has a great deal to do with our conscious experience of reality. Thus, the proposition that healing or releasing unconscious negative memories, decisions, beliefs, and traumas can greatly improve your experience is real. Here are some common hidden unconscious biases (decisions) I often encounter:

1. I am a fraud.
2. I don't deserve to succeed.

3. I am a victim.
4. Work/life is hard.
5. You must work hard and sacrifice to be successful.
6. Relationships are painful.
7. Making it to the top is for other people.
8. Other people are lucky, not me.
9. I am not good enough.
10. I should be ashamed.

If you say these things to yourself, notice your body's reaction to the statement. Does it feel correct or is it a lie? The problem is, your conscious mind can't tell you. You can only discern the effects of these biases through behavior and physical and emotional symptoms. If you are exhibiting the symptoms of stress (mental and physical exhaustion, decreasing performance, negative emotions like blame, shame, guilt, or despair) you may have implicit bias that is conflicting with your conscious desires.

Another way of detecting implicit bias is how you perceive the world. The world reflects your inner thoughts, emotions, and beliefs. In other words, you see what you look for, and we are always looking for evidence that our beliefs are correct. If you believe that you are not good enough, you will focus on all the evidence that you don't measure up, even though your belief is incorrect. You will unconsciously associate with people who will confirm that you are defective.

Here are some ways to discover implicit bias (in addition to taking the Implicit Association Test):

1. Make a chart of personal likes and dislikes. How you decide which column to put items into is probably a result of implicit bias.

2. Make a list of what you believe. Then ask yourself, "Why do I believe that? When did I decide that was true? What if it wasn't true?"
3. List the negative emotions that you experience daily, whether it is fear, sadness, anger, guilt, shame, terror, depression, rage, hate, jealousy, lust, or disgust. Then list what you were thinking immediately before you felt the emotion. That thought probably was the conscious manifestation of an implicit bias.
4. When you consider what you don't like about your life, identify what beliefs you would have to change to change your life. Any resistance to changing your beliefs would come from implicit bias.
5. Look at what you want in life and consider whether these are based on implicit bias. Even Maslow's Hierarchy of Human Needs (physiological, safety, connection, esteem, and self-fulfillment) are based on implicit bias.

Once we become aware of our implicit bias, we can decide whether to change. Until we are aware, we are like puppets being controlled by these biases.

3 | Addiction and Law

The stress and pressure of a law practice is difficult to manage. One of the more perplexing questions is whether the practice of law causes addiction or whether more people who are at risk of addiction are attracted to the practice of law. Many people who become lawyers have experienced or witnessed trauma and are attracted to the law to find justice. One thing is sure, the physical effects of stress often lead lawyers to find an escape which alcohol provides.[47] I believe that addiction is the decision to disempower yourself to the illusion of need.

Self-medication and other distractions (gambling, sex, and extreme sports) are easy and fast ways to put aside the pressures of the practice of law. During the 27 years I practiced law, the local watering hole was a welcome relief after a long day of adversity and conflict. While alcohol is much more prevalent than prescription or illicit drugs, anything that relieves the stress and constant pressure was welcome.

Bar association social events always offered alcohol to the participants, an indirect approval of its use. CLE workshops often involved overdrinking after sessions were concluded. It was like an old boys and girls club, and the alcohol and stories flowed. Alcohol generally enabled camaraderie and friendship. Good times were had by all. The problem was that alcohol has a negative, depressive effect on our psyche and often makes the pressure and stress worse.[48]

Alcohol is often used to:

- Feel comfortable in social situations
- Cope with stress
- Escape from emotional pain
- Relax
- Soothe anxiety
- Connect with peers

Other behaviors can have the same effect as alcohol. Sex, gambling, high-risk behavior, or other activities that distract lawyers from the constant high levels of adrenalin and cortisol inherent in the stress of practicing law make us feel better, at least temporarily.

Any behavior that causes secretion of endorphins and dopamine is often explored by attorneys seeking relief from stress.[49]

3.1 ALCOHOL'S EFFECT ON THE BRAIN

Alcohol triggers the production of endorphins in the nucleus accumbens and orbitofrontal cortex.[50] This produces feelings of pleasure and reward that offset the feelings of stress and pressure lawyers can experience during a long day of conflict and overwork. The problem is that the reward centers that are affected by alcohol are the same parts of the brain that help us survive through healthy behavior. Alcohol use then replaces the healthy behavior to stimulate the feelings of pleasure and reward. Eventually, alcohol will negatively impact these areas of the brain, including shrinkage of the hippocampus, which negatively impacts memory and judgment. This can lead to changes in mood and behavior, as well as make it difficult to mentally process problems.[51]

Although alcohol triggers the production of endorphins, it suppresses the production of dopamine. Dopamine is critical for brain functions like mood, memory, and movement. Heavy alcohol use may initially produce a euphoric effect, but then result in instability, irritability, depression, and memory loss.

Alcohol is often used to offset emotional pain and trauma. It will temporarily distract us from unresolved mental health issues like depression, anxiety, personality disorders, sadness, grief, low self-esteem, and social challenges. However, alcohol is classified as a central nervous system depressant and slows down brain function and neural activity. Due to its diuretic effects on the brain, alcohol can increase anxiety and stress while causing hangovers and impaired judgment.[52]

3.2 ALCOHOL'S EFFECT ON THE BODY

Chronic use and abuse of alcohol can have severe consequences on the body. Heart, liver, and digestive disease are the least of these complications. High blood pressure, coronary disease (hypertension and stroke), and other heart conditions are caused by overuse. Oral and upper digestive tract cancer are common. Cirrhosis, cancer, hepatic steatosis (fatty liver), alcoholic hepatitis, and jaundice affect the liver. Another alcohol related disease is breast cancer. The National Institute of Health has reported that just drinking one drink per day by women will increase the occurrence of breast cancer by 5–9 percent over women who don't drink.[53]

Some other long-term effects are:

- Salivary gland damage
- Gum disease and tooth decay

- Esophageal ulcers
- Acid reflux and heartburn
- Stomach ulcers and gastritis
- Internal bleeding
- Hemorrhoids[54]

There is no safe harbor for alcohol and substance abuse. Long term chronic overuse of alcohol will have tragic physical, mental, and emotional health issues. I have helped many clients learn how to drink responsibly, but "responsibly" means occasionally one or two drinks at the most. More than that will cause long term mental and physical damage. Attorneys need to find other behaviors that cause relief from stress. These are discussed in later chapters.

4 The Path to Resilience: Cultivating Mental Strength in the Legal Profession

Lawyers rely on their brains to achieve success. What many lawyers don't know is that the brain can work against us. We have an autonomic nervous system (ANS) that's made of basically two parts (although there is a third part, enteric, which is largely associated with the second part).[55]

The first is the sympathetic nervous system (SNS), which is our primary survival mechanism, also known as "fight or flight." It is unconsciously triggered every time we are confronted with threat or fear. I call this "the Warrior."

The second part of the ANS is the parasympathetic nervous system (PNS), also known as "rest and digest." This is our normal, default way of living when we are happy, creative, playful, and relaxed. I call this "the Guru."

When we talk about work–life balance, we are talking about a healthy balance of the Warrior and the Guru. For lawyers who are completely unaware of these two aspects of our neurobiology, they can easily get stuck in Warrior mode.

The physical consequences of being in Warrior mode are profound. When we are triggered and we go into Warrior mode, a cascade of physiological events occurs in our brain and our body. Adrenaline and cortisol flood our body, and we experience an addictive rush of energy. The problem is, the judgment and reasoning centers of our brain can go "offline" and we act purely instinctively instead of being rational.[56]

I struggled with weight most of my career as a trial lawyer. I usually attributed it to over drinking or snacking. I had no idea that it was the effects of the high levels of cortisol in my body 24 hours a day. I was constantly in Warrior mode. My overactive mind was always working overtime on worst-case scenario thinking. I didn't know that this was caused by my SNS being constantly activated.

I was in a constant state of fear which triggered my Warrior mode every waking hour of the day. I was afraid of making a mistake, of not getting paid, of being accused of malpractice, of not making enough money. Every time my father called me into his office, my Warrior went into hyperdrive, and I had a panic attack. I learned to fight through the panic, but it was constantly in the background.

Other symptoms of an overactive SNS are mood swings, insomnia, weight gain, anxiety, depression, irritability, compromised immune system, high blood pressure, and exhaustion. These are the same symptoms as burnout. The only way to avoid all the symptoms is to turn off the Warrior and activate the Guru.[57]

I knew nothing about my ANS in 2004 when I burned out. We didn't call it "burnout" back then, it was called a "nervous breakdown." I had been unhappy for years, trying to hold on (white-knuckling) to my practice until something could change. The result for anyone with an overactive Warrior is burnout. Burnout is our body's way of protecting itself when it gets exhausted from too much cortisol and adrenaline. It is our body's circuit breaker, which acts to keep us alive.[58]

I am the poster child for what happens when the body simply turns off. I woke up on the day after Memorial Day in May 2004 and could not get out of bed. It felt like a great weight was holding me down. The thought of going into my office was unacceptable. I had spent the entire Memorial Day weekend in a state of quiet panic trying to understand what was happening to me and why I was so depressed. It would be years before I understood. My mind and body were completely burned out and had gone into shutdown mode.

When I burned out in 2004, no one knew how the ANS and its component SNS (Warrior) and PNS (Guru) were trapping lawyers in stress responses, anxiety, depression, and negative emotions. We assumed that some lawyers were stronger than others. We recognized that lawyers who self-medicated and over-consumed were simply trying to deal with issues they couldn't handle. We didn't know the problem was neurobiological.[59]

In the unrelenting fighting ground of the legal profession, where the mental health crisis looms large, one undeniable truth emerges—resilience is not a mere option; it is an indispensable survival tool. Lawyers need to learn practical strategies that will forge an impenetrable fortress of mental strength. With these powerful tools at their disposal, lawyers will fearlessly conquer the formidable challenges that lie ahead, navigating with unwavering poise and indomitable resolve. They will be prepared to rise above the chaos and have resilience underneath their belt as their guiding light through the darkest of days.

One of the most important lessons I learned on my road back from the dark hole I dug for myself in 2004 was the fact that there are several layers to awareness and consciousness. The most important realization I learned was that I was not my thoughts.[60] What I mean by that is the part of the brain that regulates thinking is different from the part that is my awareness. I find that many lawyers are completely absorbed by their thoughts. They have been trained to research, analyze, and be logical and concise. Daydreaming and letting the mind wander are not billable endeavors.

A good metaphor to understand this is to look up at the sky. Your awareness is the blue sky, while your thoughts are the clouds that cross the sky. If you can disassociate or detach from your thoughts, you have a chance of controlling your thinking. Until we can control our thoughts, we are controlled by our thoughts. Negative thoughts, doubts, fears all can contribute to our anxiety, stress, and depression.

Resilience is the capacity to recover quickly from perceived challenges. Often this can mean detaching from what is happening in our external environment. In other words, it is the ability to look at situations as a positive event or a negative event. When we are in Warrior mode, we subconsciously view everything as negative or a threat. When we are in Guru mode, we can see opportunities and lessons.

A good example of the difference is how we react to adversity. More precisely, not only how do we react, but how do we respond? When we are in Warrior mode, we react. When we are in Guru mode, we respond. When we are in Warrior mode, we are victims. When we are in Guru mode, we are flexible, creative, and powerful. If we are not aware of these two systems in our neurology, we are bound to feel powerless.

4.1 UNDERSTANDING RESILIENCE: THE POWER TO BOUNCE BACK

Resilience is not some elusive trait reserved for the chosen few; it's a skill that can be honed and mastered. Strip it down to its core, resilience becomes the art of adaptation and recovery in the face of adversity, setbacks, and life's relentless pressures. In the cutthroat realm of the legal profession, where challenges lurk in all corners and high-pressure situations run rampant, resilience is the prized weapon that empowers lawyers to rise above the turmoil and maintain their well-being.[61]

My own experience with resilience began with my nervous breakdown. For years I had "white knuckled" my suffering, hoping that one day I would find happiness. That is a syndrome common to lawyers, sacrificing their lives in the short term for long-term wealth and success. As I found out, tomorrow never comes and happiness is not a reward for suffering.

It is a cruel joke to believe that "money" will compensate us for the suffering we can experience with the constant stress. For me, the money never made the suffering worthwhile. I did not understand that these were two completely different issues, and one does not justify the other. Happiness is not something that lives in the future. It either manifests now or never.[62]

We must find what satisfies us, what fulfills our soul. For many lawyers, that is money. My observation is that lawyers who are satisfied with money and prestige usually aren't over-stressed, and they don't need this book. For the rest of us, we must remember to build our practice around the principles which bring satisfaction to such difficult endeavors. This could be helping others, bringing change, or fighting injustice. We certainly can be well paid for our efforts and should be. However, if money doesn't satisfy your mental and emotional expectations, then we can end up like I did—emotionally, mentally, and physically exhausted.

Many times, I see lawyers who are stressed out, unhappy, overwhelmed, angry, and afraid. And these are often "successful" lawyers. I must ask myself "What isn't working?" Then I see people who are happy, self-aware, and enjoying their life. I ask myself, "What is working?" The interesting thing is, from outward appearances, there is no rhyme or reason as to who is happy and who isn't. Lack of money is blamed for many ills; however, I have met people who have no money and are full of life and love without stress. Thus, money obviously is not the key. I meet people who blame the people they love for their woes; however, I have met people who are not in a relationship who are happy and content. Whether you are in a relationship or not is not the key.

The one common denominator that is shared by all the happy people and lacking in the unhappy people is a sense of self, the acceptance of who they are.[63] The happy ones do not want to be different; they do not want their life to be different. They are enjoying what they have and don't care about what they don't have. They understand that they are constantly growing and changing. They are doing the best they can and that is good enough. They do not look for validation outside of themselves and do not care what anybody else thinks about them.

A hero can be defined as someone who does what is best for the common good no matter the risk, danger, or cost.[64] The definition of "common good" gets to be a little tricky because it is so subjective. Morals, ethics, politics, and judgment will always make "common good" a shifting ideal. I believe that the common good is anything that helps us to evolve to be divinely inspired beings who put others before us. It takes quite a bit of courage to stand up to a gossip or to your friends when you believe them to be acting against the common good. It takes more courage to be who we think we are, regardless of what public opinion might think about it.

The biggest challenge I see with people today is that they struggle with standing up for what they think is best for everyone rather than just themselves. It could be that they are afraid of losing something; there is always something that is blocking their willingness to think of others before themselves. In a metaphysical sense, they have bought into the concept that they are separate from everyone and everything else and they can do whatever they want without consequences. However, the consequences are inevitable and usually take the form of misery and suffering.

Most of us have some concept of what a hero is. What we don't have a handle on is what our story is. Even worse, we let people tell us what our story should be. Basically, our story is whatever we believe about ourselves to be true. We can be victims of our childhood suffering from emotional scars; or we can forget all our baggage from the past and focus on who we are right now. Our story is whatever we want it to be.

The biggest story of all is whether we are happy or not; whether we are the result of our past or the creation of what we believe to be true. Whenever someone asks, "tell me about yourself" or "who are you?" The answer is "MY STORY." Our past is only the training ground to be the hero of our story. If we are happy, we are the heroes. When we suffer, we are not.

The highest metaphysical/spiritual teaching is that we create our experiences, perceptions, and reality. We create this individually, as a family, community, nation, and world. The reality of a street beggar in India appears to be far different than the reality of the people who created Facebook. However, there is one thing in common between the two. They both are creating their experience for their own enlightenment. The street beggar has an illusion that their life is hard, while a multi-billionaire has an illusion that their life is easy. The amazing thing is that the street beggar may be happy, and the billionaire may be miserable. It depends on who understands that their reality is a self-created illusion, and it is all good.

For me, to be a hero in my own story means that I must take responsibility for my thoughts, words, and actions and understand that whatever I am experiencing has a purpose. The purpose of my reality and the purpose of your reality are the same. It is to be happy no matter what and to understand that we are experiencing the same thing viewed through different perspectives. If I am not getting what I want, then to be happy I must change one fundamental belief. I must want what I have. This takes a lot of discipline and courage, and some people are not able to do this. The street beggar can be happy because they accept life as it is and doesn't want anything else. The ironic thing is that when they become happy, the universe will smile, and life will change. Here is the absolute truth about being a hero; sometimes it takes more effort to be happy than it does to suffer.[65]

Sometimes being a hero means showing up and giving 100 percent of myself to whatever is happening now. It might mean letting someone else have that parking space I was waiting for five minutes to get because I can walk. It might mean letting someone in line ahead of me because they are obviously in a hurry. It might mean being kind to someone that isn't. It might mean doing everything simply because that is who we are, without expectation or desire for reward.

Where you are is the result of all your past decisions. Who you are is the result of the decisions you make from one moment to the next.[66] Probably the most valuable asset we have is our smile. When we can smile in the face of challenges and fear, we will always win and be happy. When we can smile through pain and despair, we are the heroes.

The path to resilience starts with a fundamental shift in perspective—a recognition that setbacks and challenges are not insurmountable barriers but rather a natural part of life's landscape. Embrace the growth mindset, and lawyers will find that challenges morph into golden opportunities for personal growth and learning. Armed with this mental fortitude, there's no stopping them as they forge a path of indomitable strength.

To tap into this strength and power of resilience, we must be willing to accept life on life's terms. It is not "Pollyanna rose glasses" which bring resilience, it is the ability to be grateful for life's challenges and setbacks. Anyone can be grateful for getting what they want. It is generally much harder to be grateful for getting what we don't want.

I can still remember most of the rulings that went against my clients. I remember them because I took them personally.

Whether it was a discovery motion or an appeal, if I didn't win that meant I had done something wrong. Practicing law is not the kindest environment to develop resilience.

My practice was an emotional rollercoaster. When I won, I was on cloud nine. When I lost, I was inconsolable. I was continually getting stuck in the proverbial creek mud and tripping over the smallest of pebbles on the path. This is an important aspect of resilience that I had not learned; that is, we must rise above the minutia and see the bigger picture.

One of life's most important rules for mental and emotional health is "Don't take things personally."[67] There are two parts to this rule: (1) we are not what we do, and (2) we must take responsibility for what we do. In other words, we can't make moral judgments on what kind of person we are based on our results. Additionally, we do have to acknowledge that our results are the consequences of what we do. If we don't get what we want, we must change what we do. (How we think has a great deal to do with this but more on that later.)

One of my biggest problems practicing law was I took everything personally. My victories were due to my brilliance, my losses were due to my incompetence. It didn't occur to me to think differently or act differently if I wasn't getting what I wanted. Even worse, in my mind the losses far outweighed the victories, no matter what the reality was. The satisfaction of seven-figure verdicts only lasted a moment, while the loss of a temporary matter lasted a lifetime.

Another pitfall for many of my clients is the obsession with appearances and what others think about them. This was certainly a determining factor in my depression over losing insignificant procedural issues. A client, "Louise," was a highly successful trial attorney in Seattle, Washington. She was a mid-level partner of a 75-person law firm. She saw one of my articles in the *ABA Journal* and reached out for help.

Louise was suffering from several nervous disorders, including skin rashes, acne, digestive problems, and sudden weight gain. She had just remarried and instead of enjoying life, was depressed. She felt like her partners did not respect her even though she was being paid a respectable portion of the revenues.

From the outside, Louise was a highly successful, respected, and charismatic lawyer. She wanted her name on the law firm banner, even though there were six names on there already. As usual, when we had our first session, we discovered that her real problem was rooted in an abusive childhood that kept her in fear of men.

When we went through the program, she realized that her perspective of what was going on was the problem. We changed the way she was looking at her practice into a much more positive, rewarding situation. The biggest change was her willingness to be more positive in her analysis of her situation. Rather than assuming that her name was not on the letterhead because of some disrespect, she had overlooked some clear signals from her partners that her request would be acted on at the annual partners' meeting. The firm was soon renamed to include hers.

Although she was already considered to be one of the biggest "rainmakers" of the firm, when she started looking at things with enjoyment and satisfaction, she landed some of the biggest clients in the firm's history. Her partners and clients immediately picked up on her new attitude, and it paid large dividends.

Most, if not all of her physical problems healed quickly. The cortisol and adrenaline she was constantly producing were wreaking havoc with her body. When she relaxed and started enjoying her practice, the symptoms quickly disappeared. The skin problems healed quickly, and the excess weight dropped off.

4.2 BUILDING MENTAL RESILIENCE: STRATEGIES FOR LAWYERS

There are several ways to build and increase resilience.[68] Here are a few of my favorites:

1. Mindfulness and self-reflection. Engaging in the practice of mindfulness and self-reflection is a potent weapon in the arsenal of lawyers seeking to fortify their mental resilience. By delving deep into their thoughts and emotions, lawyers gain a heightened sense of awareness. This non-judgmental and compassionate outlook empowers them to navigate the treacherous waters of stress with unwavering clarity and emotional equilibrium.
2. Setting realistic expectations. Let go of the suffocating shackles of perfectionism that plague many lawyers. Set goals firmly grounded, breaking free from the self-imposed chains of unattainable standards. By charting a course with achievable milestones, lawyers shed the burdens of needless pressure that choke their mental well-being. Embrace a healthier work–life balance, because, in the never-ending fighting ground, there's no room for anything less.
3. Seeking social support. In the throes of the legal arena, don't stand alone. Forge a formidable support network comprising colleagues, mentors, friends, and family—your lifeline to victory. Take charge and proactively cultivate this support system, providing a haven to share challenges and emotions. With comrades by your side, you obliterate feelings of isolation and stand united against all odds.
4. Prioritizing self-care. The tireless warzone is a merciless terrain, but self-care is your unbeatable weapon. Relegate nothing to the backseat; put your physical and emotional

well-being front and center. Fuel your resilience with regular exercise, a nutritious diet, ample sleep, and indulgence in activities that bring you joy and relaxation. This isn't a luxury, it's the lifeline that carries you through the storms of the legal landscape.

I find that many lawyers jump into the deep end of the "legal pool" completely unprepared to be resilient. They have excelled at everything they have ever done. They haven't had to "suffer the slings and arrows of outrageous fortune" as Hamlet lamented.[69] Their resilience has not been tested, at least not over the long run.

COVID-19 rocked even the most resilient of attorneys.[70] We had to deal with disrupted routines, lockdowns, stagnated court calendars, and learn how to practice law all over again. It literally was "teaching old dogs new tricks." The question was whether we were flexible and resilient enough to take advantage of the new opportunities that were emerging.

The good news is, resilience is a learned trait. The Cambridge Dictionary defines it as the ability to be happy after something bad happens.[71] I like to refer to resilience as the ability to thrive under adversity. Everyone has their own personal understanding of resilience, but not as many know how it works.

Here are some modern rules to developing exceptional resilience to thrive under stress. It is not something you are born with or inherit. With some focus and practice, any lawyer can learn it. There are several steps lawyers can take to be resilient. Resilience is like a muscle; it takes nurturing and use to be healthy. I have developed these steps over 20 years of observation, experience, research, and training:

1. <u>Teamwork</u>. I like to say build a team, or a "posse." Elite professional athletes rely on coaches, trainers, counselors, friends, and family to excel. Lawyers should do the

same. Resilience is a team effort. Napoleon Hill coined the phrase "mastermind group."[72] This is a group of peers that discuss problems, issues, current events, business, and personal growth. It is crucial for growth and evolution. Relationships help remind us that we are not alone, that it "takes a village" to accomplish anything. Civilization requires group effort. A successful law practice needs support and inspiration.

2. Wellness. Resilience requires a strong foundation of balanced physical, emotional, mental, and spiritual health. If any of these are imbalanced, your career may come crashing down in the face of the stress of a law practice.[73] Think of "wellness" as "balance." Get help from a competent professional for any area that may be suffering. Stress compromises our immune systems and we can suffer from many maladies which go undiagnosed, such as nutritional deficiencies, hormone imbalances, and high blood pressure.[74] All these afflictions will make the stress more acute.
3. Find the fun. One of the first things to go under stress and anxiety is the fun factor. Most lawyers would not characterize the practice of law as "fun." It is rewarding, certainly, but with all the stress and anxiety, the fun part of it is often overlooked. When we laugh, the mind doesn't care why we laugh. The benefits of laughter can offset the stress and anxiety you may be experiencing.[75] Smiling and laughing will also help the client relax and feel more comfortable.
4. Focus on the positive. You don't have to believe everything you think. You can choose not to focus on your negative thoughts and focus on positive thoughts. Transformational leaders look to neurolinguistic programming to help people transform their lives by changing their thoughts

from negative to positive. Look at what you learned by the experience rather than any adverse results. The only difference between a miracle and a disaster is choice.[76]

5. Remember your purpose. The purpose many people became lawyers is to help people. Lawyers can be seduced by the financial rewards of the practice of law. Buddha taught that desire is the root of all suffering.[77] When we focus on the good, the benefits will flow naturally. The more we serve, the more we will be rewarded. The stress of having to win to be paid can be quite severe.[78] When we focus on the help we are providing, it can greatly reduce stress. I tried to remember that I was helping people during the worst time of their lives.
6. Feed your soul. A steady diet of law practice can be lean. Listening to the problems of your clients day in and day out (and nothing else) can actually cause a traumatic response similar to PTSD.[79] Listen to music, watch an empowering movie, go outside, meditate, take a vacation. Do things that are fulfilling outside of practicing law.[80]
7. Take a break. When we take breaks (5–10 minutes) we can increase our performance. Regular breaks can maintain a high level of focus, improve our attitude, and increase our stamina.[81] It is counter-productive to focus on one thing 24/7, day after day. We will crash and burn.
8. Look for the pearls. We are questioning whether we will ever find a "new normal." Lawyers must remember that we are intelligent, trainable, and creative. No matter how stressed we might feel, our accomplishments are undeniable. A Buddhist proverb says: "dig until you hit water, dive until you find pearls." In other words, we can use the same talents and intelligence that got us here to develop resilience. We need to be the hero in our own story.

9. Forget (or at least forgive) past trauma. Neurobiology is discovering the effects of trauma on our nervous system which far exceeds common notions of PTSD. It doesn't take exploding bombshells to fragment our psyches. Childhood stress or abuse, witnessed (secondhand) abuse or trauma, and long-term stress can cause overwhelming burnout.[82] If we can look for the lesson or silver-lining in our past experiences, we can forgive our past and enjoy the future.
10. Stop self-criticism. Many lawyers regularly beat themselves up for past mistakes or losses. No one is perfect, and we must accept the fact that the concept of a mistake is an illusion. There are no mistakes, only opportunities to learn. We are always doing the best we can in the moment. The only comment we need to make about something that didn't have the result we wanted is "I won't do that again." Negative self-talk is abusive and unnecessary.[83] A great way to stop negative self-talk is to be grateful for everything in your life. You can't be grateful and self-critical at the same time.[84]
11. Don't take things personally and move on easily. Emotional maturity means that we look at life objectively and without judgment.[85] It is of no value to maintain hurt feelings when life didn't happen the way we wanted. After all, life is what happens when we have something else planned. No one lives a life with no surprises; that is what makes life interesting. If we don't get what we want, learn the lesson, and move on. We must be emotionally mature in the highly stressful legal universe, and that means rolling with the punches.
12. Don't try to teach a pig to sing. It only makes the pig mad, and you get hoarse. In other words, stop trying

to convince the world that you are right. (Although it may be our business to convince judges and jurors, this is more about being pig-headed.) There are many people with opposing opinions who will not be persuaded, and you will burn out trying to convince them.[86] Be open-minded and flexible. There are lots of ways to get your point across without having to convince people that you are right about everything.

13. Stay in your own lane. In other words, get out of other peoples' heads. Assuming what other people are thinking is a sure path to suffering.[87] Focus on your own path, and don't worry about what other people are thinking. What other people think of you is none of your business. There is a great temptation to try to manipulate people, but it is exhausting and often counterproductive. It is a full-time job to be the best person you can be and let others forge their own paths.
14. Pray and tie your camel to a tree. It is not necessary to believe in God or other omniscient beings to be a lawyer, but it helps to have faith that the world has a purpose, and you are a part of it.[88] Many lawyers put their faith in a higher power that there is a higher purpose for their work and pray to know that purpose. At the same time, they apply common sense and strive to be productive and effective. The practice of law requires effort and discipline. Keep your feet firmly planted in the real world, seek the big picture, and trust that all will be well.
15. Be kind. Sometimes when we get into Warrior mode, we forget we are human. Humans are hardwired to be communal animals; we are designed to be in relationship with other human beings. When we focus on winning and forget that we are human, we suffer.[89] Instead of combat fatigue we suffer compassion fatigue. There is no weakness

in finding ways to be helpful and kind, even for our adversaries and particularly for our loved ones. Work-life balance requires attention to our personal lives, families, and friends. When we forget that, we will burn out.

16. Don't judge (unless you are a judge). Our reality is determined in a large part by our beliefs.[90] All perception is projection.[91] When we make judgments about life or another person, we are distorting what we perceive. If we believe that life is a struggle, it will be. If we believe someone is "bad," they will appear to be bad. Our beliefs will color everything we experience. If we believe that the world is simply a blank canvas, we can paint whatever life we want. If we believe that it is a hard and dangerous place, it will be, and we will suffer. The good news is we can choose what we believe.
17. Have integrity. Be authentically you. Say what you mean and mean what you say. Be the hero of your own story and write a big one. Let the story unfold and quit trying to push a rope. Trying to make things happen (instead of letting things happen) will cause suffering and burnout.[92] Respect your body, get rest, and avoid toxic substances. Biology tells us that healthy beings live the longest and achieve the highest goals.[93]
18. Help the helpless. As lawyers, we have a great responsibility to make the world a better place.[94] Acts of compassion and service will always foster a sense of self-worth and fulfillment.[95] The problem with desire for material things is that it is never ending and never satisfied. The more we get, the more we want. The addiction to wealth and adoration is like the Midas' Touch that will cause our burnout and suffering. To bring meaning to our efforts, lawyers must stay in touch with the desire to help those who need it most.

There are other things we can do to bolster our resilience. These include:

1. Talking to someone. This can be a colleague or a mental health professional. This can be particularly challenging for lawyers suffering from burnout or compassion fatigue because they tend to isolate. We must crack through that barrier and reach out to someone we can trust.
2. Understand that the symptoms are natural and can be managed. We chose a challenging and rewarding profession. Any worthwhile endeavor requires effort, discipline, and confidence. It is the fact that we are compassionate that can make us so exhausted and conflicted. If we didn't care, we wouldn't crash and burn, but that is what makes our work so worthwhile.
3. Take more and longer vacations. Mother Teresa required her nuns to take a year off every 5 years. It is important to detach, rest, and decompress from work. Avoid working vacations. You must take a break to recharge your batteries. Weekend vacations don't count.
4. Establish healthy routines, including sleep. Although life isn't routine, we must have healthy habits, including sleep. If we must go through a lengthy period of high stress projects, be aware that you will pay the price. At least get proper nutrition and exercise.
5. Develop interests outside of your career. Have a hobby, go outside, join a social group. Go on trips. Get your mind off the stressors of your work. Have at least one endeavor that is stress-free and enjoyable.
6. Make assessments of your practice areas and adjust if necessary. If you are dealing with high stress clients and soul-sucking situations 24/7, consider changing your practice area.

7. Find experiences that give you joy and practice them daily. Have a photo album in your desk or on your computer/smart phone that you can pull out and remember fun times. Pray and meditate for brief periods regularly during the day. Breathe!
8. Think of something that makes you laugh. Humor is a powerful healing energy and can reset our mood and energy at any time. With YouTube, TikTok, and Reels, or other streaming services, we can watch funny videos whenever we need.
9. Connect with people you love. Check in with your family, best friends, and other loved ones often. They may take a little time getting used to your new habits, but connection is a key to positive mental health.
10. Think of yourself as the hero in your story. When we are confronted with people who are going through stressful and traumatic times, we must think of ourselves as noble and heroic to give us a sense of hope and wonder. Heroes don't control every aspect of their environment; they thrive on their resilience and perseverance. They know that life is unpredictable and that is what makes them heroes. Be a hero in your own mind, not a victim.

These are certainly not all the ways we can become the best we can be, but they are effective steps to that goal. Resilience is a process which requires focus and discipline. We have chosen a high risk, high reward career to achieve what we want in life.

Resilience is critical if you are in a high stress environment such as litigation or criminal defense work. Any law career that deals with traumatic or high stress situations must have strategies to balance these stressors or we will burn out.

Another word for resilience is grit. Grit seeks excellence while perfection is a mirage. Anxiety, stress, depression, and burnout are only a few of the conditions ascribed to perfectionism. *Ironically, it is the obsessive pursuit of perfection that ensures burnout.*

Grit is the nature of the process that enables us to achieve results, no matter how long it takes. It is an attitude, not the result. I remember Mohammed Ali boxing Ken Norton in 1973 and losing a 15-round split decision after Norton broke Ali's jaw in the first round. Even though he lost, everyone would agree that boxing 15 rounds with a broken jaw is the definition of grit.

Ultimately, grit is the control of what we can control and letting go of the rest. What can you control? Here is a list:

1. How we respond to fear
2. Whether you blame yourself
3. How much effort you make
4. Your beliefs
5. Your priorities
6. How much kindness you have
7. Who you spend time with
8. How happy you are
9. How and what you eat
10. What you talk about
11. What you think about
12. How flexible you are
13. How judgmental you are
14. How serious you are
15. What you focus on
16. How grateful you are
17. The memories you keep alive

When we control these things, life can be simple and enjoyable. The focus of grit and perseverance is progress, the notion of moving forward. No matter what we are trying to achieve, some days we can only manage a small step, but that is all that is required. We delude ourselves by thinking that we should be perfect when we are human.

Doing the best we can is enough.[96] Things fall into place, and if they don't in any instance, the opportunity for learning exists. We are building a life, brick by brick. When we run out of bricks, we must wait patiently until the next load appears and have faith that the bricks will come.

When I quit, I did not have the resources to deal with the stressors that kept me depressed. There was no one teaching attorneys how to have a happy, successful life no matter what happened. I was in talk therapy for years before I quit. Our traditional therapy methods typically do not address the paths forward, they examine past paths, which can be never-ending.

What we do for a living is secondary to how we live. I have learned that the issues I suffered from practicing law followed me after I quit. After I learned how to manage my blocks, life became simple again. I even returned to the legal profession, passing the bar 12 years after I quit. Grit truly is a magical gift, one which we can only give ourselves.

Be shameless. Negative self-judgment is a career killer. When we believe that we are fundamentally flawed, it is like swimming upstream 24 hours a day, 7 days a week. We aren't born that way, but too often we learn that we are unworthy from an early age.

The problem for lawyers arises when our career does not go as planned. Perhaps the business of practicing law is harder and more competitive than we realized. We experience criticism and insults and take them personally. We suffer losses or the slings and arrows of outrageous fortune. We experience great suffering and shame.

In my business of coaching lawyers in burnout, I often hear that they are mentally, physically, and emotionally exhausted.

In many ways they are often suffering from the overwhelming emotion of shame. Shame that they aren't as successful as they wanted to be, that they couldn't help their clients as much as they wanted, or were ashamed of their belief that they were failures.

As a boomer, I was often disciplined by the familiar refrain "you should be ashamed of yourself." I hope that if those authority figures had any idea of the curse they were placing on my shoulders, they would never have said it.

I also heard "you have no shame," which was supposed to motivate me to behave differently. I mistakenly assumed that shame was a good thing. Shame branded my psyche with the mantra that there was something wrong with me.

Shame can be a powerful motivator or a powerful deterrent. Being branded as "shameless," I thought I had to overachieve to prove I wasn't ashamed. As a result, I graduated near the top of my law school class with numerous honors and awards, in addition to awards as a trial lawyer.

Unfortunately, the belief that I was somehow shameful was eating away at the foundation of my soul. I believed that I was fundamentally flawed and irredeemably worthless. When I felt shame, I felt that I was incompetent and stupid. Shame is caused by an innate sense of being inherently defective.[97]

Shame also feeds into a fear of rejection, so we disconnect from people and isolate ourselves. For lawyers, we can feel shame for lack of income, clients, or success. As a result, we withdraw and experience stress and depression. For me, I burned out and quit. I did not know that shame is an unhealthy belief caused by a lack of self-worth.[98]

On the one hand, shame motivated me to excel, but on the other, it eventually caused my burnout. Since that time, I have discovered that there are steps we can take to reduce our feelings of shame and worthlessness and increase resilience and confidence.

1. Realize that shame is not the same as regret. Regret is a natural human response to having committed an action that is contrary to our values or hurts another. It is the feeling we experience when an action has harmful or unintended results. As lawyers, we can make strategic decisions that don't go as planned and regret it. However, shame is the belief that we are defective. Regret concerns the action; shame destroys the actor. Regret is healthy, shame is destructive.
2. Monitor your inner dialogue. Shame usually causes harshly self-critical self-talk. Inner statements like "I am stupid," "I never get it right," or "I am terrible at this" are common. When we talk to ourselves or think of ourselves in those tones, we immerse ourselves in negative thinking leading to anxiety, stress, depression, and burnout. More appropriate thoughts are "now that I know that, I will . . ." or "I will never do that again." Negative self-criticism is actually a defense mechanism that is intended to stop us from experiencing the pain of shame. However, if it is not controlled, it can consume us.
3. Don't overreact. When we do things we later regret or make decisions that we later learn are counterproductive, we can respond appropriately or overreact. People who struggle with shame usually overreact and "throw the baby out with the bath water." Ideally, if we don't make as much money or have as many clients as we want, we adjust our practice to bring in more clients and money. We don't just quit out of frustration and fear, which is a shame-based reaction. Life is what happens when we plan

something else, and we need to understand that we aren't going to get all that we want all of the time.

4. Disconnect from the emotion. When you are feeling shame, anger, anxiety, or stress, there is a useful exercise we can use to break the pattern of negative thinking. Sit silently and comfortably. Close your eyes and imagine you are floating a few feet above your body looking down at yourself. Imagine all of your surroundings and where the objects in your vicinity are. Then float higher above yourself until you can see your entire town or city and notice that the world is going on as usual. Enjoy the view. Then come back into your body and open your eyes, noticing that the negative feelings and fear have left your body. This meditation can be done fairly quickly, and when you practice, the process becomes second nature.
5. Recognize that shame is faulty programming. When we look at infants, we can instantly recognize their total innocence free from shame. Somewhere along the way they are taught shame. Perhaps it was a caregiver who scolded a child for a dirty diaper, or for doing something "childish." Perhaps it was an authority figure who was having a bad day and took it out on you. Perhaps it was a peer group who were cruel and unkind as only adolescents can be. No matter how we learned our shame, it is unnatural to feel that way. When we feel shame, we need to realize that there is a glitch in our psyche that we need to forgive and heal. While we may need to adjust our behavior, we do not have to destroy ourselves about it.

Shame does not have to ruin our careers and our happiness. Be aware of it and forgive the people that installed it. It is healthy at times to regret your acts; it is unhealthy to condemn yourself for them. Doing the best we can is enough.

When high-pressure situations hit, don't crumble. Embrace emotional intelligence, and you'll remain the unwavering pillar of composure and sound decision-making. No more sweating under pressure; you'll conquer challenges with ease, proving your resilience in the face of adversity. Embrace your emotions, control them, and become the master of your destiny in the legal fighting ground.

4.3 EMBRACING EMOTIONAL INTELLIGENCE: NAVIGATING THE LEGAL TERRAIN

Emotional intelligence is the cornerstone of resilience.[99] It is a non-negotiable skill that every lawyer needs. When you can recognize, understand, and master your emotions and those of others, you no longer need to play hide-and-seek with your feelings; it's time to confront them head-on.

When conflicts arise and clients turn difficult, your emotional intelligence becomes your secret weapon. Hone this power and watch how you navigate the tumultuous waters with finesse. Connect with your clients on a whole new level, unleash the power of empathy, and sharpen your active listening skills. Trust will be your ally, paving the way for a more fruitful and collaborative legal process.

The concept of emotional intelligence came on the scene about 20 years ago in studies that compared successful leaders with those who failed to succeed.[100] In talking with many lawyers about their emotional intelligence, I have found that lawyers don't pay much attention to this construct, and perhaps it is time for them to do so. In the world of business management, emotional intelligence has been found to be twice as important as intellectual intelligence and technical skills.[101] Lawyers need to integrate the characteristics of emotional intelligence into their practice and personal lives.

Awareness: Awareness is the ability to have an honest assessment of who you are.[102] This involves the traits of being totally aware of your strengths, weaknesses, values, and how you relate to others. Lawyers who are intimately familiar with these characteristics have a realistic appraisal of who they are and what they can do. I can remember being asked to be a US Bankruptcy Trustee in my district which would have been prestigious and popular.

I turned it down because I didn't think I had the organizational skills and attention to detail I thought the position required. Oftentimes lawyers get into situations that their ego failed to consider the reality of getting into. When you concentrate on your strengths and avoid your weaknesses, you become authentic. This also involves how lawyers treat each other. Many times, lawyers feel that they can only go so far with professional courtesies. Voluntary extensions of time and being courteous and kind are traits that get lost in the legal system. Lawyers need to cooperate more, especially in the family law arena.

Self-control: Self-control is another trait that lawyers need to develop. When we are calm and confident while everyone else is losing their composure is the hallmark of a wise and knowing lawyer. When we make rash decisions in the heat of the moment many times, we will regret it. I remember finding out that an opposing lawyer destroyed evidence prior to trial. My emotions enticed me to file a grievance and motions before the court. I resisted the urge and decided to let it play out at trial. I was rewarded with a million-dollar verdict. We don't always need a hammer; we can let patience be our reward.

<u>Social skills</u>: Social skills are critical. Many times, I ran into lawyers who seemed to want everyone to hate them. They were rude, abusive, and neurotic. Some recorded every conversation and meeting that they had in fear that someone would file a grievance against them. We must have some confidence and backbone as well as respect and trust.

While I could tell many stories about lawyer neuroses, what we need to see is maturity and grace. Stress is still the number one downside of being a lawyer. In my experience, stress is often caused by lack of social skills. Sometimes this involves lacking the people skills of how to be friendly and supportive. Social skills also involve building rapport with others and helping others. Lawyers are human beings and not isolationists. It is not all about the lawyer, although many may feel that way.

Oftentimes lawyers lack empathy; they could care less about what everyone else is feeling and doing. When lawyers understand everyone else, they can be so much more effective on the human side of the equation. In my opinion, being a successful lawyer is not always about winning cases, it is about being an effective human being. Knowing what everyone else is going through gives us both an advantage and an appreciation of how powerful lawyers can be.

<u>Gratitude</u>: Gratitude is probably the most overlooked attribute of any lawyer. Gratitude is the opposite of stress. Stress comes from being afraid of not getting what we want or being afraid of losing what we have. I can remember those last few months I practiced law prior to changing to another profession. I had been sued for malpractice by my client's ex, I was going through my

> own divorce, and revenues were dropping. Gratitude was hard to find in those days.
>
> I felt like I was a victim, and everyone was against me. Looking back on that now, I can be extremely grateful for my experiences. If I had known then what I know now, I probably would still be practicing law. Hopefully, developing these skills to be emotionally intelligent will help lawyers be more successful and happier.
>
> Confidence: I remember going through periods of time when everything was going against me. When lawyers experience adverse results and rulings, they need to look for the lesson. Lawyers are not victims by any means. Lawyers jumped into the pools where sharks swim. Life may be difficult at times.

Lawyers must have the self-confidence to know that life changes and adversity have a positive side to them. Lawyers need to keep their chin up and keep going. When lawyers understand that who they are (awareness) has nothing to do with results, then they control their emotional landscape.

As I coach many professionals on how to achieve success in their careers and personal lives, I have observed that after COVID-19, one quality is more important than any other in having the life we want—confidence. I have discovered that lawyers who are successful have confidence, and those who don't feel successful lack it. Confidence is ultimately more important than resilience, talent, or even intelligence. Here is why:

Without confidence, it is almost impossible to complete tasks well, make decisions, define your career, be a leader, and have work–life balance. Lack of confidence (also called self-doubt) is a soul-sucking demon that is the common denominator of burnout, stress, and anxiety.

Self-doubt causes us to overthink, make bad decisions, lose our focus, and ruin our health. Self-doubt lives in the past and is the child of perceived mistakes and failures. Even when we do well, overwhelming self-doubt will rob us of satisfaction.

If you are riddled with self-doubt and spiraling toward burnout, what can you do to turn that train around? Fortunately, there are a few easy strategies that can get you back on the road to a rewarding life.

I have found that most people who hire coaches or therapists are focused on acquiring a goal (for example, getting a promotion), power, and money. Most are focused on concrete external achievements rather than the inner qualities that are required to create them. Instead of external "work," we need to be focused on the inner work, building confidence.

We learn through experience, and it is commonly believed that we can learn more from experiences that are challenging and disappointing than those where we get exactly what we want. This is the concept of "mistakes versus learning lessons." Statistics don't always prove this to be true. The failure rate of entrepreneurs is the same for first and second startups.[103]

A larger school of thought is that we learn more from success than failure, so we ought to just succeed.[104] It seems that people who fail usually aren't paying attention, so they don't learn anything from their mistakes.[105] Confidence is an acquired trait and can be learned, and it is a lot easier to learn from what we did right than from what we did wrong. Here are some suggestions:

A. Establish Who You Want to Represent

This is the first step of creating an identity. Most "newbies" will work on whatever case their boss needs. Is that what you want? The earlier you make this decision, the easier you'll be able to accomplish this focus in your career. What are you interested in? Protecting malpractice or doctors? Pollution or green energy? Insurance defense or personal injury work? There are hundreds of practice areas to choose from. Make one yours.

B. Have a Plan

A lot of attorneys I work with don't have a plan. They became lawyers for a myriad of reasons, but they had no specific goals. More importantly, they had no backup plan for what happens if they don't accomplish their goals. Rather than sitting down with a professional to assess where they are and how to readjust, they simply get stressed or depressed. Being a lawyer is a vocation and is what you do; it does not define who you are. Having a plan gives you a road map to how to get what you want.

C. Be Honest with Yourself

I became a lawyer to please my parents. That is not a good reason to become a lawyer. Do you relish the constant give-and-take, the uncertainly of practicing law? Did you become a lawyer simply for the promise of making money or for the prestige? These are known as negative or avoidance motivations, in the sense that you are trying to avoid poverty, rejection, or lack of control. This creates stress and depression. Mental health professionals recommend that we have positive motivations to cultivate resilience. Motivations, such as the desire to help others and other positive goals, help avoid stress and depression.

D. Establish Your Priorities

I often ask my attorneys to make a list of their priorities. The stress that they experience always involves a conflict between what they want to do and what they think they must do. Listing our priorities and comparing them to how we spend our time helps us see where the conflicts are. For example, if your highest priority is family but you spend most of your time at work, you must adjust how much time you spend at work. An alternative is to spend regular time with your family, even if it is less than the time at work.

E. Find Your Voice

What is it that you want to tell your potential clients? Have a conversation with your best friend about what you want to tell your clients, and write it down (don't reveal any confidential matters). Whatever you would tell your friend is what you must tell your clients. Speak with confidence and kindness. This is the hallmark of a successful lawyer.

F. Build and Maintain a Rapport

"Rapport" is the most important word in any lawyer's world. It should be printed in 100-point font size and posted everywhere in your life. It should be on the receptionist's desk, in your conference rooms, in every advertisement, and in every room in your house. This is how we connect with everyone in our life. Do we have compassion, connection, trust? You must build rapport.

G. Find Your Platform

Be an expert. Write articles about what excites you. Talk about your talents and knowledge. Research everything about your interest area. Establish yourself on the internet. I have been writing hundreds of articles about what is important to me, and I have been recognized as an expert. Most lawyers specialize in something. Even if you have a general practice, find the area in which you really excel, and focus on that.

H. Don't Quit

It is ironic how many stressed lawyers forget that they can do the job. If a group of your peers approved you to be a lawyer, then you are worthy. If the stress and anxiety are adversely affecting your life, seek help to deal with them.

I. How to Feel in Control

Do you feel in control? Many of my clients complain that they do the best they can, and it isn't good enough. Ironically, they are in control and yet they feel powerless. I show them that they are in control, and they can change their reality. It helps to analyze what you learned when you make a mistake, even if it is just "don't do it again." Another is to understand that doing the best you can is good enough and you aren't always going to get your way. Life is about compromises and learning to live with disappointment.

J. Be Your Best

If you are a lawyer, you are competitive. It comes with the territory. It doesn't matter whether you are the best or not; it only matters whether you are happy and fulfilled. When you are happy being a lawyer, you are successful. The trick is to be confident. Confidence is the consequence of the decision that you do know what you are doing, even if you don't always get the results your client wants. Sadly, the legal profession cannot guarantee results. The only requirement is that you must be curious. Instead of wallowing in limiting beliefs and negative self-talk, be curious about what is happening in your life. Confidence comes with curiosity.[106]

Confidence is an inside job. It requires compassion, forgiveness, and love. Focus on the big picture and ignore negative self-talk. You are only as good as you believe you are. Let that belief be the firm foundation of your success.

Just because we don't get what we want or expect doesn't mean we made a mistake or did something wrong. If we did our best, but didn't get the desired result, we need to focus on what we can do differently and avoid dwelling on not being perfect. Self-doubt breeds in the space between not getting what we want and the next step. Buddha recognized this when he taught that all suffering comes from desire.

We just need to focus on the big picture. If you have forgotten what this was for you when you started, for most attorneys it is to help people. When we forget or lose sight of the big picture, and focus on our income, our status, and compare ourselves to others, doubt will generally always take over. The big picture also contains healthy amounts of self-compassion.

Are you your own best friend or your biggest critic? Do you have positive conversations with yourself? The negative aspects of your psyche are the ego, the inner child, and the inner critic. Self-compassion does not allow these negative aspects to hijack your confidence. These are the half-remembered critics, teachers, family members, and peers who were unkind and manipulative to control you. Self-compassion responds to inner criticism with love and kindness. We recognize that we didn't get what we want, but we learn and do better.

It is our choice whether we obsess on negative inner criticism or remember that the legal profession is hard and complex and very few people get to be lawyers. One of my favorite sayings is "chin up and march on." Another is "NEXT." Find a saying that cheers you up and helps you remember that you are good. If you focus on those, positive results will certainly follow.

A common cause of self-doubt is a personality defect known as "Imposter Syndrome." This is the belief that we are flawed and incompetent and one day someone will discover that we are frauds.

It is just a matter of time. We spend more time building castles in the air to fool everyone than simply being transparent and honest.

We make promises to ourselves and others which are doomed to fail. We wear different masks like disguises that are intended to convince others that we are someone more perfect than we are. We are setting ourselves up for failure and burnout. We have forgotten the big picture and have focused on external gain and validation. Instead of focusing on how we can help, we are focused on what's in it for us. Confidence is built when we show up for ourselves and others and shift our thinking to align our internal and external worlds.

The last jury trial I was involved in is a perfect example. Twenty years ago, I represented plaintiffs who claimed that a large corporate defendant had financially damaged them. I was the sole attorney for my clients against a room full of corporate defense lawyers.

After a two-week trial, the jury awarded almost a million dollars to my clients. Most attorneys would have been overjoyed. I was far from it. Hearing only my ego, inner child, and inner critic, I was so burnt out that I quit practicing law shortly thereafter. I wish that I had known then what I know now.

Theodore Roosevelt said at the Sorbonne in Paris in 1910:

> It is not the critic who counts: not the man who points out how the strong man stumbles or where the doer of deeds could have done better. The credit belongs to the man who is actually in the arena, whose face is marred by dust and sweat and blood, who strives valiantly, who errs and comes up short again and again, because there is no effort without error or shortcoming, but who knows the great enthusiasms, the great devotions, who spends himself in a worthy cause; who, at the best, knows, in the end, the triumph of high achievement, and who, at the worst, if he fails, at least he fails while daring greatly, so that his place shall never be with those cold and timid souls who knew neither victory nor defeat.[107]

If we continue to live on this planet, we must get older. There are various physiological changes that we experience as we go through the process of aging. Ignoring the legends of immortal beings that walk the planet, we all grow older physically. Genetics, supplements, a positive attitude, plenty of water, exercise, and healthy diets can help us look young as long as possible, but the best we can expect is a cause of death that reads: "died of advanced age." I remember the slogan "live fast, die young." Now that I am 70, I look forward to life after 100 years of age.

Even though physical maturity is inevitable, emotional maturity is not. I observe that most people are stuck in their emotional growth process somewhere in their adolescent years. Greed, immaturity, fear, blame, shame, resentments, anger, confusion, and suffering are all signs of arrested emotional growth.[108]

When we get stuck in our emotional development, we cease to learn how to take responsibility for our actions and our lives. We get stuck at the point of some trauma that happens in our life that we don't know how to let go of or process. Abuse, the death of a loved one, an unkind word, or a fearsome event can all cause arrested emotional development. When we stop growing emotionally, life can become confusing and overwhelming.[109]

Psychologists believe that we go through stages of development in our psychological and emotional life.[110] These stages are youth, adolescence, young adult, adult, and elder. You will notice that even though there are ages assigned to these stages, everyone is different and some people can appear to stay younger longer than others. However, we all must go through these stages eventually.

If we are healthy, our emotional development matches our physical development. I believe that we go through the emotional stages of helplessness and need, formation of personality, fear and suffering, responsibility, acceptance, and finally, peace.[111] Again, although we all start at the state of helplessness and need, these stages are not age-specific. We all have probably met people who are stuck in one of these stages or another.

Trauma and training have a lot to do with where we are in these stages. If we suffer trauma from abuse (sexual, physical, or emotional), we will get stuck in the fear and suffering stages.[112] We all know people who are stuck in this stage. With help and guidance, we can grow through the fear and suffering stage into the acceptance and responsibility phase.

When we experience fear, anger, shame, blame, guilt, and other negative emotions, it is because we are stuck in some aspect of our emotional development. Let me give you an example I experienced years ago. Monica was a lawyer in New York who I was helping after her ex-spouse died. The couple had divorced because of the years of abuse he had inflicted upon her. Someone had told her that her ex-spouse may have been schizophrenic, which may have caused him to act out all those years.

Monica had latched onto that backseat diagnosis and started blaming herself, believing that if she had been more observant, she could have gotten her ex-spouse help and saved the marriage. I was dumbfounded by the acrobatic logic she had used to feel guilty and take full blame for the divorce.

I asked more questions and discovered that she was blaming herself for the abuse she had suffered, evidence of a "battered spouse" syndrome. It was enlightening to see how she insisted that she was to blame for her ex-spouse's abuse because she should have seen the mental illness and gotten him help.

I started asking myself, "How would an emotionally mature person handle this situation?" My opinion of that was that an emotionally mature person may have grieved the passing of someone they loved for a long time but would not have taken responsibility for the abuse in the marriage. It appeared that her taking on the guilt of not being "all knowing and all seeing" was a bit like playing God.

True emotional maturity involves taking responsibility for your actions, not the actions of others.[113] If we must protect ourselves, emotional maturity means we do not feel guilty about that. If we find out something later that might have changed our earlier decisions, we do not beat ourselves up about that. We simply accept the lesson and go on about our lives as happily as possible.

I contend that to be truly emotionally mature is to be happy. Certainly, life has its experiences, and we do not need to be "Pollyannaish," but when we learn a lesson in life, we can be grateful for the insight and change our behaviors. Life is always about course corrections.[114]

We keep going on our journeys until we learn new ways of thinking and acting, and we change our course and behavior accordingly. We do not need to know everything that will happen in the future, we just need to know what we are going to do for the next few minutes.

When we want to drive from Florida to Washington State, we do not need headlamps that will light up the whole way. All we need is headlamps that will light up the next 100 feet. Emotional maturity means that when we come upon a bend in the road or an intersection, we make the necessary course correction that will get us to where we want to go. That can be all the way to Seattle or the next 100 feet, whichever brings comfort.

Similarly, emotional maturity brings happiness and fulfillment no matter what we are doing.[115] We do not need to know our life purpose, the reason we are here. All we need to know is what we are going to do for the next few minutes, hour, or day. Everything else is a great deal of speculation.

We can be happy and fulfilled being a doctor, lawyer, or shaman. We can be happy being a baker, banker, barber, or massage therapist. When we reach emotional maturity, we understand that what we do outwardly is not in direct correlation with how we feel. If we are emotionally mature, we have the discipline to do the things that keep us healthy and feeling happy and to not do the things that cause us suffering. This is the blueprint that everyone is looking for.

4.4 CULTIVATING RESILIENCE IN LEGAL ORGANIZATIONS

Creating a culture of resilience within legal organizations is essential for supporting lawyer well-being. Legal employers can take proactive steps to foster resilience among their teams:

a. **Encouraging open dialogue:** Promote open discussions on mental health and resilience, challenging the stigma surrounding these topics. Encourage employees to seek support when needed, without fear of judgment.
b. **Offering resources and support:** Provide access to mental health resources, employee assistance programs, and wellness initiatives. Support staff in balancing workloads and promoting a healthy work–life integration.
c. **Providing training and education:** Offer resilience training and workshops to empower lawyers and support staff with practical tools to manage stress and enhance emotional intelligence.

In this quest for resilience, lawyers must remember that building mental strength is an ongoing journey—a continuous process of growth and learning. By embracing resilience, lawyers can equip themselves with the tools to navigate the challenges of the legal profession with courage, determination, and a renewed sense of purpose. In the next chapter, we will explore the significance of self-care in promoting lawyer well-being and sustaining mental resilience.

In my work with lawyers, helping them avoid stress and build resilience, I am noticing that many are starting to send their support staff to me for help with the same stress, anxiety, and burnout that attorneys experience.

Even though lawyers may be more and more conscious and aware of the issues they are facing, their staff's suffering may be difficult to spot. Sometimes lawyers can be accused of malpractice for what their staff did or failed to do because of being overly stressed or burned out.

Lawyers should not only be looking for the symptoms of burnout in their own lives, but they also need to watch for it in their employees. The things to watch for are:

- They lose their sense of humor and stop smiling
- They are irritable and impatient with their coworkers
- They appear to be tired and may have trouble getting to work on time
- Their productivity decreases
- They lack focus or seem to have trouble concentrating
- They complain more than usual
- They complain of headaches or stomach aches or take more sick leave
- Unexplained weight gain or loss
- They blame others for problems at work
- They often seem distracted
- They have no life outside of work
- They are working more and more overtime
- They act bored
- They are disinterested in conversation
- They have developed a negative attitude

There are some aspects of the workplace that tend to increase stress and burnout. When you do personnel reviews (and you should be doing these regularly), be sure to inquire about the following:

- Whether they feel supported or isolated at work
- Whether their workload is realistic for the long term
- Whether they need anything to be more productive
- How they feel about their co-workers
- What changes they would like to see (if any) in the workplace
- Whether they are feeling any unusual stress or anxiety
- Whether they have any concerns that are impacting their work
- Whether their work is monotonous and boring and if so, what they would like to be doing
- Whether they are getting enough breaks and time away from work

If you see the warning signs of burnout or if your employee does not feel supported or challenged at work, you should consider offering a mindfulness program at work. This could include counseling, meditation, music, breathing practice, stretching, exercise programs, nutrition training, and team-building activities. Workplaces that encourage a healthy work–life balance often experience less turnover and more job satisfaction with employees.

If you have an employee that is exhibiting the signs of burnout, reach out to them. It is always more expensive to replace a good employee than to rehabilitate them. From a management perspective, be sure that you are realistic and compassionate in your management style. Make sure that you do not burden them with:

- Unrealistic deadlines or schedules
- Long periods of work without breaks
- Threats of disciplinary actions for mistakes
- Lack of praise and recognition
- Micromanagement
- Lack of leadership

It is important that you meet regularly with employees who may be suffering from stress and burnout to monitor their work satisfaction and interest. Let them know you care about their well-being and value their contributions. Encourage them to speak up if they are feeling overwhelmed and exhausted. Give them opportunities to decompress, and make changes to their workload if necessary.

Employees that want to work in a law firm (high-stress) environment should be cherished and nurtured. Replacing a long-term employee is many times more expensive than getting them the help they need. If you are experiencing high turnover, consider reviewing what you are demanding of your employees and what kind of support you are giving them. Just as lawyers need support and guidance about burnout, so do their employees.

It is important to remember that support staff can be affected by stress and anxiety just as much as attorneys. I regularly get calls from attorneys who are concerned about their secretaries or paralegals whose effectiveness or competence begins to wane. Just as attorneys can be negatively affected by the tragedies that happen to their clients, the attorney's staff can also suffer.

Paralegals and secretaries can suffer from the same syndromes as lawyers, such as secondary trauma disorder, PTSD, secondary PTSD, chronic stress, anxiety, and depression. Oftentimes they care about their clients as much as attorneys and can internalize and identify with their clients' struggles.

I was called by an attorney in Boston to help his litigation paralegal, a woman named Betty who had worked with him for 20 years. She had started making uncharacteristic mistakes and errors in judgment. She had started missing work due to sickness and ill health. She often complained of "brain fog" and couldn't seem to focus. It was obvious that she wasn't sleeping well, and she was suffering from mood swings and bouts of anger.

After working with her for a couple of hours, it was clear that she was suffering from the symptoms of secondary trauma disorder and an overactive SNS (Warrior mode). After explaining to her why she was experiencing stress and anxiety, it was easy to give her some techniques to turn off the Warrior mode and turn on her Guru mode. She immediately reported sleeping and feeling much better and quickly returned to her normal self.

The ABA has published supporting materials that may be helpful in establishing a supportive culture. See Section 6.6, below.

5 The Power of Self-Care: Nurturing Well-Being in the Legal Profession

In the fast-paced and demanding world of law, the practice of self-care often takes a back seat. However, neglecting self-care can have profound consequences on the mental and emotional well-being of lawyers.[116] In this chapter, we delve into the transformative impact of self-care and explore practical strategies for lawyers to prioritize their well-being amidst the rigors of their profession.

5.1 UNDERSTANDING SELF-CARE: A VITAL COMPONENT OF RESILIENCE

Self-care encompasses a vast array of practices that place paramount importance on our physical, emotional, and mental well-being. Let's get one thing straight—it's not a luxury or a frivolous indulgence. Self-care is a nonnegotiable foundation for maintaining resilience and conquering the relentless demands of the legal realm. Lawyers who wholeheartedly embrace self-care understand that nurturing their own well-being enables them to better serve their clients, approach their work with unwavering clarity and purpose, and ultimately thrive in this challenging profession.

A trendy focus these days is "self-love."[117] Many attorneys fail to realize that they can't really love their work or anyone else if they don't accept, respect, and honor themselves. Even now, with countless self-help books, webinars, coaches, gurus, religions, meditation, and social media posts galore, we can't seem to fully embrace this concept. The truth is, we can't be happy until we accept ourselves. We can't be satisfied until we honor ourselves. We can't be balanced until we respect ourselves. We can't achieve true success until we appreciate ourselves.

When I started practicing law back in the 1970s, I assumed (like many of my colleagues) that having a law license would make life easy and wealth assured. What I found was that I had jumped from the baby pool of academia to the shark-infested (pun intended) deep end of the pool of the business of practicing law. Competition and the struggle to make "the big bucks" was a painful reality.

We were told that we had to "fight," we had to "sacrifice," we had to devote time, energy, and money to create a successful career. I will never forget a conversation I had with the senior partner of the law firm I joined after I passed the bar exam. He told me that a successful career was based on a three-part foundation—devotion to (1) work, (2) family, and (3) community. He was correct to a certain extent; a successful career does require attention to those three concepts. However, what he neglected (and what attorneys often neglect) is a devotion to self.

Mental and emotional health depends on the alignment of your conscious mind and subconscious mind.[118] When you have goals, plans, expectations, or dreams that are not supported by your subconscious mind and you suffer from an unhealthy opinion of yourself, your hopes and dreams will never be realized.[119] If your subconscious mind believes that you are unworthy, an imposter, a loser, or a fraud, it is impossible to love yourself and achieve your goals. If you are suffering from deep emotional or mental trauma, you won't achieve homeostasis (work–life balance) for yourself.

When your subconscious mind is overly critical, fearful, and traumatized, it is almost impossible to hear the voices of inspiration, intuition, and resilience. Connection with your intuition, inspiration, and resilience are often the talents that separate the truly successful lawyers from the rest of the pack. How do you know which cases will be successful? How do you know who to trust and rely on? How do you make decisions that can make or break a career? Do you have that "sixth sense" that gets the big client or the big win?

When you are disconnected from your inner voice of self-assurance and confidence and can only hear the voices of your inner critic, inner child, and ego, it is impossible to achieve your goals. In my opinion, this is the true cause of burnout. It is exhausting to listen to the constant chatter of your self-criticism. You wouldn't let a stranger treat you or your loved ones that way.

There are several concepts that directly bear on the conflict of the conscious and subconscious minds:

1. <u>Motivation versus behavior</u>. Why we do the things we do is just as important as what we do.[120] Motivation is broken down into positive and negative attributes. We behave based on selfish or altruistic purposes. For example, do we practice law because we want to fix something that we believe is broken or do we practice law because it is admirable and just? Do we strive mightily because we are afraid of being poor or because we enjoy helping people?

   This distinction can make all the difference in how you view yourself and your career.[121] Lawyers who are motivated by service and compassion achieve satisfaction and fulfillment, while lawyers who are primarily motivated by fear and selfishness are never satisfied because making money does not feed their souls. It only keeps the wolves at bay, but the wolves are always there, lurking on the sidelines.

Lawyers must examine what motivates their work and sacrifice. If they can decide to work to help others versus feeding their fear of poverty, they will become more fulfilled and satisfied and may possibly not burn out.

2. Accept thyself. All perception is projection. We can see only what we are looking for. If we believe that we are flawed or an imposter projecting a persona that is false to appear competent and confident, our cognitive bias will find evidence that this is true. Our subconscious minds are powerful and create our own reality. Studies in implicit and cognitive bias show that our unconscious beliefs shape our perceptions of the world.[122]

   If we experience gratitude, forgiveness, understanding, acceptance, intuition, and inspiration, we will experience self-acceptance. I began to believe that life is simply a series of experiences that teach us how to love ourselves, not a battle to be fought every day to avoid ridicule and ruin. When I accepted the fact that I am just as valuable as anyone else, no matter what I had experienced, and that I matter and deserve success, I began to achieve my goals.

   If we accept ourselves, we can deal with our inner critic, inner child, and ego in healthy and inclusive ways.[123] Self-criticism does not have to be a constant distraction. When I started to accept myself, imagine my surprise when I stopped living in the past filled with regret and resentment and could experience joy in the moment and excitement for the future. I embraced the concept that I was a perfect version of myself at every stage in my evolution.

3. Self-confidence. Self-acceptance includes confidence. According to the dictionary, confidence is as "a feeling of self-assurance arising from one's appreciation of one's own abilities or qualities." The phrase "appreciation of one's own abilities or qualities" is also the definition of self-acceptance.

   When we are stressed, afraid, depressed, and on the road to burnout, we focus on everything that is going wrong. We forget that we have achieved a high level of success merely by becoming licensed attorneys. We must focus on our talents and successes and learn from our experiences. By focusing on these aspects of our lives, we can achieve a positive outlook and be resilient. Focus on "I can," not on "I can't."

4. Practice. I always wondered why it is called "the practice of law." I believe we practice what we want to excel in. Do attorneys practice, or do they simply "do"? I also believe that it is indicative of knowing that we never achieve perfection; we do the best we can.

   Practicing law presupposes that we always can improve. If our "practice" is not where we want it to be, we must strive to do better, not beat ourselves up about where we are. Do you practice giving arguments? Do you learn how to behave like a successful lawyer? Do you practice your people skills, your confidence, your client relationships? Or do you just wing it, hoping for the best? How many times have you gotten in front of a mirror to practice your arguments or explanations?

   I suggest that "self-acceptance" recognizes that we can always do things "better," and we have the confidence to find out how. We continue our legal education, but do we go to wellness seminars? Do we seek out ongoing life education or ongoing relationship education?

> I have found that practice in any of these areas will vastly improve your practice of law (and life).
>
> The practice of law is a spiritual calling.[124] Having a spiritual practice is just as important as any other practice.[125] We must remember the big picture and that we are here to serve, not just make money.[126]

It's time to challenge the prevailing narrative that glorifies overworking and sacrificing personal needs as a misguided badge of dedication and success. We must rewrite this narrative, empowering ourselves to recognize that self-care is not an obstacle to greatness but a catalyst for sustained excellence. Let's debunk the myth and reclaim the narrative—self-care is an integral part of the journey to resilience, and it is high time we embrace it unapologetically.

The myth of short-term sacrifice for long-term gain needs to be reexamined. My colleagues and I were indoctrinated with the belief that if we devoted long hours to our practice in the beginning, somehow it would pay off later down the road.

The problem I discovered with this theory is that it is a myth with no basis. Hard work only serves to create more opportunities for more hard work. There is no magic alarm clock that will go off after 5, 10, or 20 years that tells us we won't have to work so hard.

The harder the work we perform, the harder we must work. As we become more successful, the more responsibility we will acquire. Not only will we have to focus on what we do, we will be given responsibility over others. Once we make partner, we must make enough revenue to pay overhead and our own needs. This is the natural evolution in a lawyer's career.

As I discovered, if we do not have strategies to balance the long hours and responsibilities of a law practice with our personal needs, we will crash and burn. It is inevitable. The longer we keep cortisol and adrenaline in our system, our mind starts to crave the rush they produce, and we start manufacturing reasons to stay in Warrior mode.

Ironically, we can get addicted to the adrenaline and cortisol, and when it leaves our system when we relax, it feels uncomfortable. We can't relax because our body is craving adrenaline and cortisol. If we don't know what is happening in our brain and body, we begin to subconsciously create problems to activate the Warrior and the associated chemicals that are produced.

Looking back on the end of my days of practicing trial law, I understand that my subconscious mind was forcing me to make decisions that I would later regret to create excitement in my life. I would forget appointments, double-book clients, or act in ways that were uncharacteristic to create drama. I did not learn until years later this was my brain seeking excitement to boost adrenaline and cortisol in my system. When I thought I was happy, it was just a low grade of anxiety. I didn't know what happiness was.

Somewhere I formed the belief that suffering and sacrifice were noble. Along with that, I was taught that the only way to become successful was with hard work and sacrifice. The long hours, missed children's events, and insomnia became some kind of perverse badges of honor. If I had admitted to myself that these sacrifices were detrimental to my well-being, I would have had to admit I was wrong. All I knew was hard work; that is what I was trained to do.

What I have discovered through scientific research, education, and training is that success has nothing to do with hard work. It has everything to do with smart work, collaboration, and mentoring. Pain should not be part of a plan for success; rather, joy and fulfillment are the real components of success. Without joy and fulfillment, practicing law is just a stressful job.

I have adopted the belief that happiness is an inside job. Initially, I bought into the illusion that sacrifice and long hours would be rewarded at some point. These sacrifices created a lot of stress because I not only was trying to please my parents who wanted me to be a lawyer, I was trying to convince myself that doing something I didn't like was good for me. I hadn't wanted to be a lawyer; that was my parents' dream for me.

What I didn't understand is so often missed by many human beings: happiness is a choice, not a reward. I kept looking for happiness by making more money, winning more cases, and becoming respected in my field. Being happy is a state of mind, not something you get. We can be happy and make a lot of money, just like we can make a lot of money and not be happy. Making a lot of money has nothing to do with being happy. "Doing" has nothing to do with being happy.

Being happy has nothing to do with what I am doing at any given moment. Being happy has nothing to do with getting what I want. Being happy is the conscious decision to be grateful for whatever is happening at any point in time. Being happy is the byproduct of being in Guru mode, feeling safe and relaxed.

5.2 THE PILLARS OF SELF-CARE: STRATEGIES FOR LAWYERS

A. Managing Workload and Boundaries

Let's face it—burnout is a real threat in the legal world. But don't fret, there are practical steps to shield yourself from its grasp. Set clear boundaries, both with yourself and your clients, to avoid spreading yourself too thin. Learn the art of delegation when needed, and don't hesitate to prioritize downtime for relaxation and rejuvenation. Remember, your well-being is not negotiable.

One of the basic tools attorneys can use to make their life more balanced is to calculate how much revenue they should bring in. If they are starting out their careers, they may be given goals as to how much time they need to charge to (a) stay employed or (b) be promoted.

For many firms, this is written in stone, and the attorney must decide whether they can commit such a large portion of their life to work to the detriment of their personal life. Most lawyers are eager to be fast-tracked to partnership, but they do not realize the toll that will take on their personal life.

Lawyers must take responsibility for their personal lives if they want theirs to succeed. I assumed that my wives would support my desires to work hard and make money, but after enough lonely nights, they wanted out. The negative fallout from all the stress I was feeling from working long hours at a job I didn't want was causing stress in all of my relationships: as a spouse, a parent, a colleague, and a friend. Underlying all of it, I didn't like myself very much.

B. The Power of Mindful Awareness

Mindfulness isn't some abstract concept—it's a game-changer in managing stress and nurturing your emotional health.[127] Embrace mindfulness practices like focused breathing, meditation, and grounding techniques. These tools will help you stay present during high-pressure situations, maintaining your composure like a seasoned pro. It is time to take a deeper dive into the ANS.

This is where awareness of our autonomic nervous state is critical. Are we in Warrior mode or Guru mode? Are we pumping adrenaline and cortisol into our body or endorphins and dopamine? If we are not aware that we are in Warrior mode and we are full of adrenaline and cortisol, that becomes our new normal. When it becomes our normal state of being, our fight-or-flight response becomes our constant companion, and rest and relaxation become uncomfortable.

Many people wonder why they are stressed when their life is successful. Most of my clients are professionals who have created financial abundance and status in life, yet they are unhappy, disillusioned, and burned out. I have discovered that this is due not only to constant worry and pressure, but also because of ignorance of how the ANS works.[128]

Many people are familiar with the fight, flight, or freeze response to a perceived threat. What they don't know are the intricate functions of the ANS that can affect our perception, beliefs, and reality. It is not a matter of controlling our thoughts and emotions because our conscious mind has no control over our ANS.[129]

The ANS controls many of our bodily functions without conscious thought. It regulates our breathing, digestion, circulation, and endocrine systems, so we don't have to constantly remember to perform any of those functions. Our ANS is principally located in the medulla oblongata and spinal column (brain stem), the oldest part of our evolutionary brains, and spreads throughout our body through our central nervous system.[130]

As our brains evolved from reptiles, it added the temporal lobe (memory, behavior, language, hearing), the occipital lobe (vision), the parietal lobe (reading, body sensations, orientation), and the frontal lobe (problem solving, reasoning, speaking, voluntary motor functions). These appeared approximately 200,000 years ago, while the brain stem was developed millions of years ago.[131]

The ANS is divided into parts, including the SNS ("Warrior") and the PNS ("Guru"). The Warrior is primarily concerned with survival, as it is usually referred to as "fight or flight." The Guru is concerned with contemplation, creativity, and relaxation and is usually referred to as "rest and digest" or "feel safe" response.[132]

This anatomy lesson is important for two reasons: (1) our experience of life is far different when we are activating our Warrior (stress) versus our Guru (creativity),[133] and (2) we can control which system is activated, so we can change our experience from pain to pleasure.[134] I call this "brain hacking." Over the last 20 years, neurobiologists have done extensive research into the correlations and effects of each system of our minds and bodies.[135]

An important feature of the Warrior response and the Guru response is how they are activated. The Warrior response is activated primarily by sensory organs perceiving threat (fear) while the Guru response is activated by feelings of safety and peace.[136] Over the long term, too much Warrior will result in cognitive decline, while the Guru supports cognitive functioning.[137]

Biologically, the Warrior response triggers the hippocampus to feel fear and signal the adrenal glands to secrete adrenaline and cortisol. This is good for life-threatening situations because this reroutes all our body's resources to our muscles and survival. The problem is that when the Warrior response is activated for long periods of time, our reduced higher-brain functions make poor decisions, which keeps us locked in the Warrior response. Furthermore, we are prone to see threats that do not exist and keep our Warrior response activated.[138]

The warning signs of excess cortisol in our system are probably familiar to many lawyers:

- Fatigue
- Irritability
- Headaches
- Digestive problems such as diarrhea, constipation, bloating
- Anxiety
- Depression
- Weight gain
- Increased blood pressure
- Decreased libido

I experienced all these symptoms before I burned out. I instinctively knew that it was related somehow to all the stress I was feeling. What I didn't know was it was due to my ANS on Warrior overload.

Stress comes in many forms and produces many symptoms. Symptoms range from worry and irritability to restlessness and insomnia, anger and hostility, or sensations of dread, foreboding, and even panic. I would often lose my temper over nothing and get upset at even the most trivial things. I had no idea that this was caused by the mental stress I was under which was, in part, due to being stuck in Warrior mode.

When we can activate the Guru response, our bodily resources go back to support higher brain functions and we can relax. This is where we can connect with our inspiration, imagination, and intuition (the three *I*'s) and can feel safe. Feeling safe is the origin of feeling loved and the basis of civilization, connection, and communication (the three *C*'s). The Guru response triggers the hippocampus to signal the relevant organs to secrete dopamine, serotonin, melatonin, endorphins, and oxytocin, the "feel good" and "love" hormones.[139]

When you compare the two systems, spending too much time with the Warrior response will lead to isolation, stress, anxiety, depression, and a compromised immune system. According to Maslow's hierarchy of needs, humans require esteem, belongingness, and safety, and physiological needs for basic physical, emotional, and mental health.[140] If not met, humans will feel anxiety and stress and suffer. It is impossible to meet these needs if the Warrior response is activated for long periods of time.

Conversely, when the Guru response is activated, not only can our basic needs be met, but the conditions for growth and self-actualization and enlightenment can be achieved. The Guru response can help create art, music, dance, common purpose, group identity, justice, and civilization. In fact, while the newer parts of the brain (temporal, occipital, parietal, and frontal lobes) made civilization possible, they do not adequately function unless the Guru response is activated.

I have seen remarkable changes in the quality of life of my clients when they switch out of the Warrior response and into the Guru response. The stress and overwhelm associated with work, relationships, or health-related pressures melt away, and solutions present themselves. I burned out in 2004 and now realize it was caused by an overactive Warrior response (I called it DEFCON 5). If I had known about the Guru response then, I most likely would not have burned out.

It is remarkable how these same practices were developed in the East without any knowledge of the ANS or the Guru response. Monks and yogis simply knew by trial and error that these activities produced feelings of bliss, awareness, relaxation, increased consciousness, and well-being, as well as releasing negative emotions such as fear, anger, regret, guilt, and shame. Ironically, Western medicine is finally catching up to Eastern spiritual practices.

I incorporate all the activities listed above in my daily routine, and now I rarely feel stress or negative emotions. The longer I can activate my Guru response, the neuroplasticity of my brain will change to support my Guru response, "programming" my brain to think and believe in positive ways.[141]

By learning how to activate the Guru response, we can return to our natural state of safety and belonging. By doing this, we can achieve communication, connection, and civilization with inspiration, imagination, and inspiration.

Through all my training, education, and research, I have discovered several techniques that help turn off my Warrior state of mind and activate my Guru response. The mindfulness techniques mentioned above—breathing, meditation, and grounding—are good for reducing stress. There are even better techniques to relax. Here are a few.

1. *Ho'oponopono*

I am a licensed attorney. I am also a certified Advanced Ho'oponopono Teacher and Practitioner. The reason that I became interested in this little-known spiritual practice is that I wanted to learn an easy way to manage stress, anxiety, and worry. It is also a great way to increase emotional maturity, manage emotions, achieve mental clarity, and feel positive. It helped me to realize a deeper purpose and application to law, which I have been sharing with legal professionals ever since.

An ancient Hawai'ian practice dating back centuries, Ho'oponopono burst onto the international scene by virtue of the book *Zero Limits* by Dr. Joe Vitale and Dr. Ihaleakala Hew Len in 2007.[142] Dr. Hew Len tells the story that by using Ho'oponopono, he helped heal an entire psychiatric ward for the criminally insane in the Hawaii State Hospital without meeting any of the patients. Even though these claims have been contested, thousands of people have embraced the practice to heal their emotional and mental challenges.

The practice is based upon the concept of "*total responsibility*" for everything that surrounds us—confession, repentance, and reconciliation. Also known as "All perception is projection," the belief proposes that everything that we perceive not only exists outside of us, but also exists inside of us as well. If we perceive something in our outer world that is a problem, it is caused (or created) by a problem within us in our inner world. Happily, if we perceive something in our outer world that is positive, that is caused by something positive inside of us as well.

Ho'oponopono means "correction" or "to make right." It recognizes that all illness or problems in the world are caused by the transgressions of others or of the person who is suffering.

The practice is simple enough. It involves the use of four statements (mantras) below that are to be repeated as many times as possible by the practitioner.

The order of the statements is determined by the practitioner; whatever feels correct is perfect. The object is to say this mantra over and over until it creates new neural pathways and becomes second nature. As Drs. Hew Len and Vitale would say, "You become the prayer."

It is important to make these statements with positive intention. The quality of the emotion used will increase the effect of the practice. The four parts of the mantra are as follows:

a. **I love you**. The "you" here refers to both the participant and the perceived problem. You can only love someone as much as you love yourself. This not only is quantitative, it is also qualitative. If you don't love yourself, or your definition of love is flawed, it is likely your perception is skewed and creating the problem. You must feel love, affection, and compassion for yourself and the problem. As the famous poem by Kent Keith says, "Love them anyway."

b. **I'm sorry**. This does not mean blame, guilt, and shame. Victimhood is not allowed. This means that we take ownership and responsibility for what we perceive. It also takes ownership and responsibility for whatever needs to heal inside of us. The first step in any conflict resolution is to admit that there is a problem. It is the acknowledgment of the problem that allows our compassion to liberate our hearts and psyche to heal. When we accept responsibility, we are empowered to heal. If we say, "This is someone else's fault," we disempower ourselves.

c. **Please forgive me**. Self-forgiveness is the great cleanser. It allows us to let go of our burdens and struggles. For lawyers burdened with guilt or regret, self-forgiveness is oftentimes the healing that they need. The request is to whoever we seek guidance from or pray to, either internally or externally. Ultimately, we are the source of our pain and suffering, and we are the only ones who can heal that pain and suffering. This also does not mean that we forget the lessons we have learned from our experiences. Even with forgiveness, we grow.

d. <u>Thank you</u>. Gratitude is one of the magic emotions that overrides all other emotions. When we practice gratitude, we can heal any internal suffering. To be thankful for all that we experience is one of the most powerful prayers in any religion. We are given life to learn and grow emotionally, mentally, and spiritually. When we are truly grateful for our experiences, we not only grow, but we heal any misunderstandings or misconceptions.

This practice of Ho'oponopono is both meditative and healing. Practitioners report relief from negative thoughts, emotions, and behaviors. By focusing on these four principles of love, compassion, forgiveness, and gratitude, we can create new neural pathways and thought patterns that transform our experience from negative to positive. If this practice helps any problem in our exterior lives, that is an added benefit, for its primary purpose is to heal the practitioner.

Attorneys can certainly use this in several applications in their professional and personal lives. Remember that when a problem arises, you are made aware of it to heal some aspect of yourself. The aspect is usually subconscious, and you are not aware of it. The problem can be a difficult client, finances, opposing counsel, adverse rulings, disagreements with colleagues, or problem family members.

Simply acknowledge the problem and say the four phrases above with the intention that you will heal. Say the phrases one at a time, slowly. The more you can feel the associated emotion (love, compassion, grace, and gratitude) as you say each phrase, the more quickly it will heal.

Interestingly, the practice of Ho'oponopono has been approved by the Hawaiian judicial system as an acceptable form of mediation.[143] If it is good enough to settle litigation, it is good enough to settle a stressed psyche.[144]

2. *Vagus Nerve*

Research has shown that the vagus nerve has a great deal to do with how we feel. It is probably the most important nerve in our body because it is the information highway between our brain and our internal organs. Neuroscientists have discovered that activating the vagus nerve will activate our Guru response.[145] When we are stressed or anxious, this reduces the energy flowing back and forth between our brain and organs, it deactivates the vagus nerve, and we feel "bad." When we activate the vagus nerve, we activate the Guru response, and we can create a feeling of relaxation and calmness.

There are several techniques to activate the vagus nerve[146]:

- <u>Facial nerves</u>: One of the easiest ways to activate the vagus nerve is to activate our facial nerves. Our facial nerves are connected to our cranial nerves (C7), which are connected to the vagus nerve. To do this, take a seated position with your eyes looking straight ahead and hands shoulder high at the edge of your peripheral vision. Look to your left as far as you can and count to 60. Then look to your right as far as you can, and count to 60. Repeat this until you feel a sense of calmness and relaxation. It should only take a couple of cycles. You may even yawn, which is a signal that our Guru response has been activated. A simpler way to activate our facial nerves is to simply smile.

- Cold water: Splashing cold water on your face or taking a cold shower does wonders to reboot your mind. When you find yourself anxious, tense, stressed, or depressed, put cold water, a cold washcloth, or a cold towel on your face or head. You will feel better instantly.
- Humming or singing: The vocal cords are situated near the vagus nerve, and activating the vocal cords can activate the vagus nerve, creating a feeling of relaxation and calmness. This is why singing and humming can be so satisfying. When you sing in the shower, there is a reason it makes us feel so good. When monks chant "*OM*," there is a reason it calms them down and clears their heads. These activities activate the vagus nerve, resulting in the Guru response and a sense of calm and relaxation.

3. *Hakalau*

Hakalau is a Hawaiian term that refers to "expanded vision."[147] It is a technique developed by Huna healers in Hawaii to refocus the mind and create an "open-mindedness" to allow the brain to create new neural pathways. It involves using peripheral vision to create new thought patterns.

Hakalau is extremely simple to achieve. Sit with your spine upright and looking straight ahead. Raise your hands with palms facing forward above your head. As you continue to look straight ahead, wiggle your fingers, and separate your hands until they are at the edge of your peripheral vision. Then raise and lower your hands along the edge of your peripheral vision as you continue to wiggle your fingers.

You will notice an almost instant change in your mood and stress level. You will feel calm and relaxed. Continue to move your hands along the edge of your peripheral vision until you are free from anxiety and stress.

4. *Meditation*

Meditation is often misunderstood and overly complicated by practitioners. Many people believe that meditation requires the cessation of thought, and mindlessness. Mindlessness may be a goal for some, but that is not what is required for successful meditation.

I first started meditating in 1970 with a technique called Transcendental Meditation. It was introduced to the United States by an Indian guru named Paramahansa Yogananda. Students were given a secret word (called a "mantra") that they focused on while they "meditated." My ultimate understanding is that meditation is merely the observation of and detachment from your thoughts.

Whenever you do any meditation, the first step is to "get grounded and centered." Relax and imagine there is a cord of light or energy from your feet going into the ground to the center of the earth. You can also imagine the cord branching out like the roots of a great tree, connecting you to the earth. Feel gratitude for the support Mother Earth gives to us, nurturing us and supporting us. Then feel a cord of light or energy running from the top of your head to the center of the universe, or to the God of your understanding. Feel the inspiration and magic coming down from this source of energy into the center of your being.

There are lots of different techniques for meditation once you are centered and grounded. Included are:

- <u>Breathing meditations</u>: This is the focus on various breathing techniques (see section 5.2.B.2 above), which allows your mind to relax and clear. There is the box breath (4-4-4-4), relaxing breath (4-4-6-4), rapid breath (to energize), and slow breath (to calm yourself). You can close one nostril for the inhale and close the other to exhale. All these techniques are known as pranayama yoga, and many different examples can be found online. Other breathing techniques include:

- **The "ha" breath.** When you exhale, make a dynamic exhale with the throat, forming the word "ha." It can be a short, explosive exhale or a long, slow exhale. This will produce a calming effect and warm the body.
- **The cooling breath.** Fold your tongue lengthwise, forming a tube. Inhale through the tube until your lungs are full, and hold for the count of eight. Then exhale through your nose. This will cool the upper body, head, neck, and upper digestive track system.
- **Humming breath.** As you exhale, hum like a bee. This will activate the vagus nerve and clear the mind.
- **Walking meditation.** As you are walking, focus on your body and your breath. (You might want to initially have someone with you, as you can forget where you are). How do you walk? How do you breathe as you walk? Asking yourself these questions will help ground you and get into your body, clear the mind, and focus your thoughts.

- Body scan meditation: This involves getting quiet and still and scanning your body for tension or stress. When you find stress or tension in your body, focus on relaxing that area of the body, releasing the tension or stress. You can ask yourself what the geometric shape of the tension is, what color the tension is, how big it is, how heavy it is, etc. This will help you associate with the tension. When you exhale, let the tension and stress flow out of your body along with your breath.
- Blue dot meditation: Take a piece of paper with a blue dot the size of a quarter drawn or printed on it and put it on the wall at eye level when you are sitting down. Place

your chair a few feet from the wall and focus on the dot. Whenever a thought enters your consciousness, refocus on the blue dot, and let the thought flow through your mind. Do not resist it, just let it go. Eventually, you will be able to focus on the blue dot without any thoughts intruding on your meditation.

- <u>Space between thoughts meditation</u>: This meditation is especially effective to help people meditate and clear their minds. Instead of focusing on a thought, focus on the space between thoughts. Initially, this space may be a nanosecond, but the more you focus on the space, the longer it will get. Try to go for 10 seconds, then 20 seconds, then 30 seconds. Eventually, you will be able to still your mind for minutes, or as long as possible. This will release any negative thinking and allow you to relax.
- <u>Red balloon meditation</u>: This meditation is especially good when we are feeling negative emotions such as anger, fear, stress, anxiety, guilt, or shame. Locate the emotion in your body. Where is it, what shape is it, what does it feel like? When you have located it, imagine a red balloon floating in front of you. Place the negative emotion in the balloon, with all other negative emotions, and imagine the balloon floating up and up until it goes into the sun and is consumed. The negative emotions will be gone.
- <u>Mantra meditation</u>: One way to stop negative thinking (especially habitual negativity) is to focus on positive words.[148] Ho'oponopono is one such way to focus on other thoughts. I have been practicing mantra meditations for 20 years. I have been taught many sacred spiritual mantras, which I use in my daily meditations. You can choose any positive affirmation or word that is meaningful for you and just repeat it in your mind. Let

neuroplasticity do its thing. The more you repeat the positive word or thought, the deeper it will be ingrained in your thinking patterns.[149]

5. *Health Is Wealth*

Your physical well-being is the backbone of your mental resilience. Make time for regular exercise, nourish yourself with a balanced diet, and don't skimp on quality sleep. These are not optional extras—they are the key to your cognitive function and overall health.

It is important to have regular blood tests to check on your endocrine system. The years of stress and anxiety wreaked havoc on mine. I had my hormones checked and discovered that I had hypothyroidism, which was linked to high cortisol levels.[150] This also contributed to my feelings of exhaustion, confusion, low libido, and low metabolism. When I started taking hormone replacement, all those symptoms were reduced.

It is common knowledge that stress has a negative effect on our health.[151] Plato said, "Exercise would cure a guilty conscience." Exercise is also something the whole family can enjoy. Walking, running, playing pickleball, swimming, and all forms of cardio/anaerobic exercise can help families bond. Exercise is good not only for your body, but it is also excellent for your mind.

Regular exercise will bring remarkable changes to your body, your metabolism, your heart, and your spirits. It has a unique capacity to counter depression and dissipate stress.[152] This has been verified in clinical trials that successfully used exercise to treat anxiety disorders and clinical depression. If athletes and patients can derive psychological benefits from exercise, so can you.

Exercise reduces cortisol and adrenaline while increasing feel-good chemicals such as endorphins, dopamine, and oxytocin.[153] When you reduce cortisol, you feel more energetic and begin to lose weight, which increases your pride and self-confidence.

Inexorably entwined with exercise, nutrition plays a huge role in our mental health.[154] A proper diet can offset and relieve depression.[155] Being healthy requires more than just exercise. I have the number 23 tattooed on my shoulder to remind me that anyone can go to the gym for an hour, but what you do the other 23 hours makes all the difference. As one lawyer put it, "No amount of exercise can compete with what you put in your mouth each day."[156]

Everyone's physical needs are different, and it is far outside the scope of this book to outline what you need nutritionally to maintain optimal performance. I encourage you to research what your body needs and to create a food plan to enhance your life. There is a lot of debate over what healthy eating is, but everyone agrees that eating healthy is better.[157]

Four months ago, due to chronic pain, I discovered that my seemingly healthy diet was causing a host of digestive issues, including a leaky gut, depleted enzyme levels, and inflammation. I consulted a nutritionist, and now I eat a strict diet of raw, plant-based vegan food. It is a difficult food plan to say the least, and it is amazing how biased our thinking is against that kind of food plan. Incredibly, the most vocal critics of my choice are my friends who are doctors. I think everyone should know that medical doctors are not trained in nutrition.

I have lost 35 pounds in three months and feel the best I have felt in years. I sleep better, think clearer, and my pain has stopped. I strongly suggest that everyone research the foods that they eat and the effect of how the food is prepared. I will leave it at that.

6. *Strength in Connections*

You're not in this alone. Cultivate meaningful relationships with colleagues, friends, and family. These connections are more than just social niceties—they're vital emotional support systems.[158] Simply venting to another person can reduce cortisol in our bodies. We are hard-wired for social bonding.[159] Our brain activates mirror neurons that reflect the moods and emotions of people we communicate with. When we are with people we trust, we feel safe, we activate the Guru, and we are at our best.[160]

Studies on solitary confinement have shown the destructive effects of solitude and lack of social support.[161] Lean on your trusted friends and colleagues, share your experiences, and find comfort in knowing that you're never facing the challenges of this profession solo. Together, we can weather any storm.

I have researched the positive advantages of mastermind groups in achieving goals, accumulating wealth, and mental and emotional well-being. The personal growth arena advocates the use of mastermind groups to improve our results, outlook, and moods.[162] Mastermind groups can not only be an emotional support system, but also a think tank, a sounding board, and a brainstorming juggernaut. There are numerous legal mastermind groups on the internet.

I have long advocated having a "posse," or a group of friends and colleagues from various backgrounds for support. I join as many mastermind groups that I can find that support my efforts. They are invaluable.

7. *Spirituality for Lawyers*

Historically, there has always been an interrelation between law and the battlefield.[163] As I remember from my history classes, the modern judicial system replaced trial by combat to resolve conflicts. In a civil society, it became much more efficient and fairer to foster a system where no one died, and we elected our peers to decide who was telling the truth or at least who should win a conflict. Unfortunately, trial by combat still exists on a global scale as is recently seen in the Ukraine and the Middle East.[164]

Spirituality has been described as the gift that comes in the box called religion. In other words, the concept of spirituality consists of the core elements and concepts which bring us peace and calm, happiness and satisfaction, confidence, and fulfillment. Sometimes spirituality has been equated to the five human values of (1) truth, (2) right conduct, (3) peace, (4) love, and (5) non-violence.[165] These values can sometimes seem far removed from the practice of law.

People are motivated to become lawyers for various reasons, including money, prestige, power, and success. Many go into the legal profession with the dream to make a positive difference in the world, to protect the innocent, the environment, and to help businesses thrive. After they graduate from law school and pass the bar exam, they sometimes discover the harsh realities of the practice of law resulting from competition and the need to win. This can cause stress and disillusionment for those who didn't realize that making money at the practice of law can be difficult. This is where spirituality can help.

When we look at the five human values, these are the attributes that are our highest nature. When lawyers fall away from these values, lawyers are acting against their highest nature, and this will cause suffering at some point in their lives. If we apply these principles to our legal practice and personal lives, the practice of law can become a source of pride and enjoyment.

- <u>Truth</u>: When I practiced law, I sometimes faced the dilemma of disclosing facts that I thought would negatively affect my client's case. Lawyers walk a thin tight rope between being an officer of the court and keeping the confidences of a client. Once I had to withdraw in mid-trial because my client insisted on testifying to facts I was convinced were not true. I reviewed my ethical responsibilities and had to make the hard decision of withdrawing. I know I made the right decision; the Federal judge told me years later that if I had not withdrawn, he probably would have reported me to the State Bar. If a lawyer is confused about that, be sure that seeking the truth will always have a better result than trying to avoid it. Lawyers usually know when they are hiding the truth, and if they do it may become a great source of stress. Telling the truth is more than a goal, it is a way of life.

- **Right Conduct:** Being a lawyer is simply a role we have chosen to play. Lawyers have to "play by the rules and obligations" of being a lawyer in order to benefit themselves and society. People who think that they "don't have what it takes" to be a lawyer are looking at the microscope from the wrong end. What lawyers need to practice is being the best person they can be while they go about the business of being a lawyer. Lawyers must envision what their most divine nature is as a lawyer and then be that. It is more than being moral or ethical, it means living the most virtuous life possible. If people cannot be virtuous, it will be very difficult to be stress free and confident. Lawyers need to stop judging others; they need to concentrate on being a role model for the rest of society.
- Peace: Faith in the divine and in oneself is the source of mental peace. Lawyers must let go of excessive desires and unreasonable expectations. The source of all suffering is wishing that our life was different. Desiring more money, more success, more clients, more fame is the source of

most stress for lawyers. Blaming themselves for an unexpected result is not productive. Lawyers are egotistical enough to take the blame for everything in their lives and criticize themselves harder than most. The circumstances that surround lawyers are always the result of some decision made in the distant or recent past. Lawyers can't blame others for their fortune or misfortune, life is an experience that lawyers have come to enjoy. Lawyers get emotionally attached to their cases and suffer when the results are a disappointment. Mental and emotional discipline is the only way to avoid suffering.

- **Love:** True love is not to be confused with lust. Love is only the desire to help others. When lawyers serve their community and clients with honor and compassion, all of society benefits. When lawyers are focused only on the reward for their actions, they will suffer. True love is the relationship between lawyers and everyone else, it is the force of nature that brings peace and tranquility to all lawyers do. Kindness is the hallmark of love, and every lawyer can use a large dose of kindness in all of their affairs. When lawyers focus on what they can do for others, instead of the opposite, life gets much more rewarding.
- **Non-violence:** Most people, including lawyers, do not understand that committing violence against another is committing violence against oneself. Violence is not only physical violence, but also an unkind thought, word, or action. When we gossip, criticize others, or get angry, we are committing violence. Lawyers can help their clients see positivity in their life and to focus on what is beneficial in their world. I fear that lawyers have made everything in life someone else's fault and they live off of making their clients victims instead of enabling them to

learn from their experiences. No matter what happens in a client's life, sue someone else. Lawyers need to help people take responsibility for their lives instead of making them victims.

When lawyers meditate and contemplate the application of these values in their lives, they will find stress and confusion leaving their lives. Their relationships will become healthier, and they will enjoy their work more. This is a full-time job, no matter what we do as a profession.

8. *Set Your Daily Goals*

We often have a list of daily "to-dos" for our business. Many people understand the importance of setting goals for their business.[166] The question is, do we have a list of daily "to-dos" for our personal lives? We have already talked about brain "hacks" to get us out of the Warrior response and into the Guru response to erase stress and toxicity from our lives.

a. Personal Goals:

Here is a list of personal goals that we can add to our daily routine to transform our stress into success:

- Have a short gratitude list that you can review throughout the day to remind us how lucky we are.
- Help at least one person every day without expectation or reward.
- See how many people you can get to smile.
- Hug at least one person every day.
- Look at the sky for at least five minutes.
- Walk barefoot on grass (or get an earthing mat).

- Listen to nature.
- Be silent enough to hear your heartbeat at least once a day.
- Say thank you to everyone you talk to and be grateful for life.
- Be aware of your breathing for at least five minutes.
- Listen to a recording of a child's laughter.
- Laugh out loud at least once a day.

b. **Smart Goals:**

As with any goal, whether it is personal or professional, we must be "smart" about creating and accomplishing the goal.[167] The acronym "S.M.A.R.T." stands for:

- Specific

Many of us have non-specific goals that probably took the form of New Year's resolutions. I want to lose weight, be healthier, get in shape, or work less. These are rather vague and have too much uncertainty to know if you have accomplished them. You must establish what exactly is to be done, who is going to do what, and how you know it is accomplished. What are the steps that you have to take to accomplish the goal? Make the goal as itemized as possible.

- Measurable

This involves having an objective, quantifiable standard by which you can determine if the goal is accomplished. There must be some way to track progress and establish benchmarks to demonstrate your progress. How will you know you are making progress? What are the numbers you will use? If you want to be healthy, it is easier to make the goal to go see a doctor than use "health" as a parameter.

- Achievable

This is otherwise known as the reality check. Sure, we all want to weigh our optimum weight, but in two weeks it is usually not achievable. We must ensure that we give ourselves enough time to realistically accomplish the goal and the goal is within our reach given enough time and resources. If we must break a larger goal down into smaller chunks, that is better than some amorphous ideal. By breaking down the goal into steps, we can maintain our enthusiasm and marshal our resources.

- Relevant

Another aspect to the reality check is to make sure the goal is in alignment with your beliefs and expectations. From time to time, I am tempted to go back to school to get another degree, but given my age and schedule, a master's or doctorate program is probably beyond my grasp at this point. The "why" is just as important as "how." In the personal realm, you will need to have some idea of who you are and how you want to change.

- Time Deadline

According to author Napoleon Hill, a goal without a deadline is just a dream.[168] Without a deadline, it is difficult to measure progress. When you have broken down the steps to accomplishing the goal, be sure that the deadlines are short enough to require action and long enough to allow completion.

9. *Be Like Buddha*

The idea of Buddhist lawyers is not new. The more important question is what Buddha would do in various situations that lawyers often find themselves. That question is much more profound and rich for contemplation. We can find clues of how Buddha would behave in his teachings and philosophy, and how it relates to the reality of legal practice.[169]

First, Buddha was all about mind control. The control of your thoughts, your emotions, and your beliefs. The very essence of the new concept of "Mindfulness" is the awareness of the mind and how it functions.[170] Mindfulness is recognized as being beneficial to how we experience life and practice law.[171]

When I went to law school, the first lecture I attended was by a famous law professor. He pompously informed the students in the room that the primary purpose of law school was to teach us how to think properly. He declared that all the poets in the room should be sad because when law school was done with them, they would never write poetry again. That "old school" approach has gotten us to the crisis we are experiencing today.

Legal thinking is primarily subjective and biased to a position that is favorable to your client. One of the criticisms of lawyers is that they don't stand for anything, they just like to argue. They will argue just as hard for one side as the other. It is an issue of debate and rhetoric, not what will bring the lawyer peace and happiness.

Even today, 20 years after quitting from an active law practice, I find myself approaching issues from a "win–lose" perspective, only now I am the client. I was trained to analyze the strengths and weaknesses of beliefs and behavior to win my case, and I often think about what I am about to do or say from the perspective of how that will sound to a jury. This does not mix well with bliss and happiness.

I do find that Buddhist principles can be applied in a law practice.[172] Buddhism proposes four noble truths and eight ways to achieve those truths. The Four Noble Truths are (1) life involves suffering, (2) desire and ignorance are the source of suffering, (3) suffering can be healed, and (4) the way to end suffering is the Eightfold Path.[173]

In order to end suffering we must apply the Eightfold Path which is (1) an accurate understanding of the world, (2) right motivations (avoiding attachment, hatred and harmful intent), (3) right speech (avoiding lying, gossip, rumors, unjust criticism, rudeness, and abusive words), (4) moral behavior (no harm, sexual misconduct, substance abuse, and have compassion), (5) moral livelihood (your profession should not harm others, respect the rights of others and be of service), (6) have a positive attitude and action, (7) be present (be aware of what we are doing), and (8) focus on what is important to us.[174]

Buddha would not be concerned with whether his client was going to win or not, Buddha would be objective and truthful. Buddha was, more than anything else, a realist. He understood that everything he did had a consequence (karma), and he should do no harm. Sometimes lawyers seem to lose their conscience, they shut off that tiny voice in their head that what they are doing may cause harm if the money is right.

The issue is not whether people can be successful, for Buddha was a cunning businessman. One of the most famous Buddhist icons is a sculpture of a title to one of Buddha's monasteries that cost millions of dollars. Buddha knew how to make money, make loans, and charge interest. However, Buddha was not greedy, he made money to support his monasteries. Buddha would charge a fair price for his services, but not an exorbitant one.

Buddha would not be stressed about anything. He would have been the center of the storm of whatever was storming around him. Lawyers need to be more like that, keeping themselves and their clients calm, centered, and grounded and not letting their emotions run away with them.

For example, imagine that Buddha had a meeting with a new client who was emotionally distraught over a business or personal matter and the client wanted to crush the opposition.

Many lawyers would familiarize themselves with the case, perhaps into the early morning hours, sacrificing their personal time to make a good impression. Buddha, on the other hand, may give the material a quick glance and then pay attention to his emotional health and positive thinking.

When he met with the client, Buddha would not make promises or inflame the situation further by recommending Armageddon. Buddha would be looking for compromise and peaceful resolution for the best result for the client, keeping in mind that a long and expensive trial may not be in the best interest of his client.

Buddha would exhibit two traits that are rarely found in law offices: compassion and empathy for the opposition. Mediation courses often recommend that lawyers try to understand what the opposition is thinking and feeling so that a resolution can be achieved because a resolution is always preferable to conflict.

The most important aspect that Buddha would bring to the table is to teach his client the practices of meditation and contemplation so that the client could be objective and open-minded to solutions. Buddha would not be swept up in the emotions of his client and he probably would understand that perhaps the client was perceiving the conflict irrationally. Buddha would encourage the client to bring his emotions and his rationality into balance so that justice could prevail. Buddha understood that justice had nothing to do with winning, it had to do with emotional health.

The core of Buddha's teachings was wisdom, ethical behavior, and contemplation with a nod to the changing nature of reality. How this would show up in a law practice is that winning and losing is not important, the well-being of the client and service to the community would be most important. The well-being of the client would have nothing to do with winning, it would be the resolutions of his problems.

The service to the community could be either volunteering or pro bono work. I regularly won awards from my local state bar for pro bono work, and I would proudly display them in my law firm's lobby. They would mysteriously disappear, and I would find them in a closet somewhere. When I asked the senior partners why they didn't want community service displayed in the lobby, I was told that the firm didn't want the public to know that we offered free legal service. I find that attitude common among law firms.

Buddha may or may not have earned a lot of money from practicing law. It would not have been important to him. However, he was a good businessman, and he would certainly have earned enough to accomplish his other goals of serving his clients and the community. The satisfaction of his legal practice would not have had anything to do with how much he made, it would have been how much he helped his clients. Perhaps every lawyer should have the same goals.

10. *Dealing with Unpleasant Lawyers*

Let's face it, we have all had to deal with overly aggressive, rude, and unpleasant lawyers at some time in our careers. Many state bars have enacted rules regarding professional behavior, but human nature is what it is, and not every lawyer is accommodating and flexible. Some lawyers are overly litigious, fighting at every hedgerow and making the practice of law more stressful than necessary.

These lawyers are probably the source of the public's low opinion of our profession. According to the 2023 Gallop Poll, for integrity and honesty, lawyers only ranked higher than journalists, advertisers, business executives, car salesmen, Congress, and telemarketers.[175]

When we must deal with lawyers who are particularly unpleasant or combative, there are some steps we can take to rise above the fray and achieve some equilibrium in our interactions. My observation is that there seems to be more of these lawyers in the family law arena, which only made a difficult situation worse.

During my 20 years on my spiritual path post-burnout, I have found some fundamental principles which work wonders with irascible lawyers.

a. **Awareness:** Whenever we must deal with unpleasant people, we must be aware that there is something within us that has attracted that person to our attention so that we can heal that part of us that attracted that lawyer. Another way of saying that is we create our reality from our beliefs, our biases, and our prejudices. Instead of taking offense at the other lawyer's behavior, get curious and ask yourself "how am I like that?"

   When I am completely honest with myself, I must admit that I engaged in some gamesmanship from time to time with opposing counsel. When I felt like they were being uncooperative or less than transparent, I could go down that road as well. What we resist outside of ourselves the most are reflections of the most hidden parts of ourselves that we dislike. When opposing counsel is behaving inappropriately, it reflects what Carl Jung called "the Shadow," the aspects of our subconscious that we fear the most.[176]

   Examine your negative emotions about dealing with the lawyer and let them go. Anger, anxiety, fear, or other negative emotions are all signals of something within us that needs to be healed. Do the Red Balloon meditation (above) and relax.

b. **Acceptance:** Develop a sense of humor. Have compassion that these lawyers are probably suffering from stress, negative emotions (especially fear), and may be headed for burnout themselves. When I realized that I did not have to react to their rudeness and aggressiveness, I could start to problem-solve. We don't have to go to every fight we are invited to, and we can simply accept that they are hurting and not let that affect our mood. After all, we knew practicing law wasn't going to be easy going in. Be better than them.

c. **Willingness:** Don't resist. Get curious. There are always going to be unpleasant people in our lives, how do we deal with unpleasant people in general? Have we ever really thought about having a strategy to deal with unpleasant people? Do research, find strategies, and don't take it personally. Just because they are unpleasant, that doesn't mean that we must suffer. How they act has nothing to do with us, how we react is totally under our control. Look for the lessons we can learn in this situation.

d. **Gratitude:** Be grateful for everything that comes into our lives. People who have mastered their life are grateful for both the things we like and the things we don't like. Being grateful for unpleasant people may seem like an impossible task, but it goes a long way in eliminating anxiety and stress.

   Look for things you can be grateful for about that asshole and what you can learn from them. We all have teachers of how to be, and teachers of how not to be. When we can see how we may be like that person, we can change. The interesting thing is when we change, they will change, or at least our perceptions of them will change. Practice saying "thank you" either internally or out loud. It may not change their behavior, but it will confuse them.

e. <u>**Expansion:**</u> Whether we like it or not, when faced with difficult lawyers we must raise our game. We can get motivated to do better, be more inventive, get out of our rut, problem solve, and get better results for our clients. Whenever I dealt with "that lawyer," I took it as a challenge to do more research, be more creative, and find new ways to persevere. Unfortunately, I did not have this book to help me overcome the other challenges in my practice, but getting a good result with a difficult counsel on the other side was especially rewarding.

5.3 REDEFINING SUCCESS: A PARADIGM SHIFT FOR LAWYERS

In the cutthroat world of law, it's time for a paradigm shift—a redefinition of what success truly means for lawyers. Let's break free from the old belief that success demands endless hours and relentless sacrifice. It's time to broaden our perspective.

Success isn't just about ticking off cases won or clients satisfied. It's about finding fulfillment and well-being in every aspect of our lives. So, let's embrace a new definition of success—one that includes personal happiness, self-care, and a healthy work–life balance.

We need to let go of the guilt that often accompanies taking care of ourselves. We are valuable professionals, not machines programmed for overworking. Redefining success means realizing that our worth isn't measured by the number of hours billed or how little time we take for ourselves.

It's time to prioritize our well-being, recognizing that a healthy, thriving lawyer is a more effective and resilient lawyer. Let's redefine success and create a new standard—one that brings genuine fulfillment and lasting satisfaction in both our professional and personal lives. Together, we can thrive in this demanding field while also nourishing our own well-being.

5.4 EMBRACING THE JOURNEY TO SELF-CARE

As lawyers embark on their journey to self-care, they must recognize that it is an evolving process. Embracing self-care requires self-compassion and patience as old habits and societal pressures may challenge the commitment to well-being.

By nurturing their mental and emotional health through self-care, lawyers can build a solid foundation for resilience, empowering themselves to face the demands of their profession with strength and vitality. In the upcoming chapter, we will explore additional strategies to foster a supportive and nurturing legal community, promoting the well-being of lawyers at every stage of their career.

Happiness is the result of a kind heart. Therefore, to develop happiness, one must develop a kind heart. My experience in this world and the experience of many people I have met on the spiritual path includes emotional and physical trauma. Something happens to us that frightened us, hurt us, and made the world a scary, unsafe place.

My experience is that these traumas hardened my heart like a callus or scar tissue that my body forms for protection. Even more subtle wounds are created when we experience something that we don't like. These wounds are often dismissed or ignored because they don't necessarily hurt. These more subtle wounds might cause frustration, irritation, anxiety, or stress, but are accepted as part of everyday life.

As I trudge the path of happy destiny toward spiritual freedom and light, it is my duty to remove these calluses, bruises, or wounds on my heart. This is necessary to allow my heart to open and to expand my consciousness. I am convinced that happiness cannot be logically reached; it must be experienced through our hearts. It is reassuring that one of the oldest belief systems in the world incorporates this belief in the form of the statement that happiness can only be reached through a kind heart.

I often contemplate: what is a kind heart? So far, the best conclusion I can draw is that a kind heart is a heart filled with compassion, awareness, and acceptance. There is no room in a kind heart for resentment, resistance, anger, or any other "negative" emotions. I further believe that these painful energies are the result of what the Buddhists call lazy or habitual thinking.

I call it "worst case scenario thinking." As a former attorney I often imagined what the worst-case scenario would be in a trial and plan accordingly. This defense mechanism was very useful as a lawyer; however, when it spilled over into my personal life it caused great suffering.

One of the most important steps in developing a kind heart is to understand that we are not our thoughts. When we have thoughts of a hurtful or painful nature, we must not condemn or criticize ourselves for these thoughts. We must simply accept them as passing thoughts. When we dwell on these thoughts or resent them ("resent" means "to think over and over") we are building thicker and thicker calluses and scar tissue on our hearts.

Another important step is to understand that we create our realities for the specific purpose of becoming enlightened. When life does not suit us, we must look for the message we are telling ourselves by creating something we don't like. Some common themes I am witnessing these days include: (1) money has nothing to do with happiness; (2) companionship is not necessary for happiness; and (3) common sense is more important than spiritual sense.

To develop a kind heart, we must understand that we do not need money, soulmates, material things, and 13 spiritual diplomas to be happy. We simply need to accept the fact that we are exactly where we are supposed to be—going exactly where we are supposed to go.

In my experience, one of the most damaging illusions and lies that we tell ourselves is that we are not living the life we are supposed to live, that we are somehow doing something wrong and that we are victims. Whenever we experience stress and anxiety it is because we believe something is wrong somewhere in our life. This leads us away from a kind heart because a kind heart is flexible and pliable enough to understand that everything is imperfectly perfect.

A great exercise for those anxious moments is to sit still and breathe into the heart. Imagine that when you inhale, you are sending light and oxygen into your heart (not the lungs). When you exhale, imagine that you are exhaling all illusions and misunderstandings that hurt out of your heart. It is amazing how fast relaxation comes when one does this.

It is not so important that we be kind to others as it is to be kind to ourselves. There is no need to feel guilty, ashamed, stressed, or anxious when we have a kind heart. A kind heart is like a loving parent observing a child who is angry or frightened and knows that everything will be alright. The child (us) does not know everything will be alright, but the parent does. When we can feel the feeling that everything will, somehow, work out, we can relax and enjoy life.

The payoff for having a kind heart is the inevitable effect that people will gravitate to us. We must understand that some people will be kind, while others will project their anger and fears all over us. When we have a kind heart, we do not take offense at these people, we understand their pain and have compassion for them. This is how we can develop compassion for others, by being kind to ourselves.

Ultimately, we come to the realization that everyone is simply a reflection of the thoughts and feelings we experience.

When we can respond with kindness to everything, to the thoughts, emotions, events, and people that we like and dislike, bliss will be ours.

As I journey through life, I contemplate the times I was truly filled with joy and the times I was not. I have this itch that never seems to be satisfied. It is the itch to fight. I am a fierce competitor, and I love nothing better than a good argument or debate. I guess that is why I was such a successful lawyer for 27 years.

Most lawyers can separate the argument from the cause. By that I mean a lawyer can argue passionately for a position and then turn around and argue just as passionately for the opposite position. When you are arguing with a lawyer, be forewarned that they don't care who is right, they only love the battle.

Despite protests to the contrary, I find most "spiritual" people have a position and will defend it passionately, even if it means to argue about equanimity or bliss. That is like rolling in dead skunks to get clean.

Anyone who is interested in spirituality and changing their life for the better must detach from the fight, and as Buddha instructed, find the middle way. Some of the most passionate debates (arguments) I have engaged in were about spiritual concepts. How absurd is that? It's a trap laid by the ego to keep us addicted to the fight within all of us.

Here are some things I believe that people need to realize to transcend this trap:

1. <u>Melodrama</u>: We are addicted to melodrama. We convince ourselves that we are victims, and we need to tell everyone about it for our mental health. Who did what to whom is a favorite conversation, even in spiritual circles. Ideally when people get together, we can be silent and just enjoy each other's energy. We don't need to talk at all. But where is the perverse fun in that?

We thoroughly dissect everything that has happened "to" everyone and then judge it aloud or silently against our own melodrama. It seems to be human nature. Look at the current election campaigns. I can't remember so much vile and vituperative propaganda pouring out in the news and on the internet. Instead of emphasizing what is positive and unique about themselves, it seems that our consciousness level requires that we spread lies and half-truths about the other candidates. We end up electing the "least-worst" candidate, not the best. No wonder we are so disappointed in administrations. We always elect who we deserve. The bottom line is, we argue for sport and entertainment, not for necessity. And as in the case of many things, including campaigning, the melodrama serves to distract us from the real issues at hand.

2. Judgment: We love to judge everything and everyone in our lives. Originally, we learned to judge for survival, whether to run, fight, or relax is one of our most primitive thought patterns. As we got civilized, we eradicated most of the daily threats, so our egos had to invent some other threats to have something to do.

   We invented the concepts of "right/wrong," "good/bad," "better/less," and "enough/not enough" to keep us busy. The business of "thought" is just a game to keep our ego busy and to validate its existence. What most people don't and can't realize is all these concepts are illusions and aren't real.

   What we perceive isn't necessarily real either. All perception is, in fact, projection. Which means that we see what we want to see. Being a trial lawyer for 27 years taught me that 10 people can witness the same thing, and you will get 10 different stories about what happened. We rarely say to ourselves, "Wait a minute, I'm an advocate for my own way of thinking, and what I am perceiving may not be accurate."

3. My way or the highway: We get so enamored with our perceptions that when challenged, we don't know what to do. We run away or fight; this is our primitive nature and usually comes in the form of forgetting to breathe. When we are threatened, our primitive nature is to hold our breath and our fight/flight reflex kicks in.

   We must be very aware of our bodies to prevent this reflex action, especially whether we are getting enough oxygen to our frontal cortex to be able to analyze and respond, rather than react. I had a very tough childhood and suffered from PTSD for many years. That was a tough one to crack because every time I heard a loud noise, especially people shouting, I went into panic mode. I had to learn to focus on my breathing and life returned to a less threatening experience.

4. Never try to teach a pig to sing: By that I mean why do we try so hard to convince everyone that we are right. A great exercise is to calculate how many minutes a day we think about how to convince other people we are right. To be candidly honest, that is what I am doing right now writing this article.

   The highest spiritual teachings would have me sitting in a cave allowing other people to experience their life and stop trying to show them a different path. Many people leave breadcrumbs for others to follow, thinking that their journey's experiences will help others live a happier, more fulfilled life.

We all are at different levels of consciousness and awareness, and I had to learn that some people will understand what I am saying, and others will not. That is the reality of what I do. Rather than argue harder, I simply wish those who disagree a pleasant journey. There is one caveat I would give to "never try to teach a pig to sing," and that is "until they are ready."

5. Attachment: We are attached to many things, including comfort, pleasure, abundance, beliefs, thoughts, and our identity. The spiritual leaders of all ages say that when we let go of who we think we are; we will find who we truly are. People not only fight others to defend their attachments, but they also fight themselves most of all. It is impossible to find peace and tranquility if we are waging a war inside our heads over who we think we are versus who we think we should be, or whether life is fair or not.

   What we must do is detach from all of the things that make us suffer, like comfort, pleasure, abundance, beliefs, thoughts and our personality. I realize it sounds counterintuitive to suggest that one detaches from things that feel good, but if you expect to feel good all the time you will wind up suffering when you don't. The only way out of that nasty jar of homemade, sorry ass jam is to take responsibility for the suffering we cause ourselves. We never suffer because of external circumstances; we only suffer because of what is happening in our minds.

6. The scoreboard: Many arguments are carried for decades and are fueled by the past. I can remember the most frustrating thing about my second marriage was that my wife would bring up stuff that allegedly happened 20 years ago (my first marriage only lasted a couple of years, she didn't have a boatload of baggage to dredge up). Who wants to carry that around for 20 years?

   I would have no idea what she was talking about, and apparently no amount of good behavior would wipe the slate clean. More damaging, however, is that we do that to ourselves. We just can't seem to let the past go.

> We are constantly beating ourselves up about stuff that may or may not have happened. Regret eats us alive. We are constantly feeling sorry for ourselves because of stuff that may or may not have happened.
>
> We are hurt when people don't acknowledge us like we think they should and we shut down when people trigger our core issues (abandonment, rejection, not enough). Then we blame ourselves for stuff we had no control over. If there is a hell, it is between our ears. No wonder we fight with other people; we are duking it out all the time in our minds. Besides, ultimately, no one cares if you're right, except you.

What do we do? We must detach from our beliefs, our thoughts, and our circumstances. When we find ourselves in the middle of a battle, we must imagine ourselves on a mountain top looking down on the situation. Taking a deep breath, we can focus on what is the kindest thing we can do in the moment. No one ever regrets being kind. When we focus on how we can be and remember that we have a choice to go into battle or not, we can totally rise above the fighting, bickering, fear, and suffering. The simplest solution of all? Detach from yourself, your ego, and your mind and just be kind.

6 Fostering a Supportive Legal Community: Building a Culture of Well-Being

The legal community is not merely a collection of individuals practicing law; it is a collective force with the power to shape the well-being of its members. In this chapter, we explore the significance of fostering a supportive legal community that prioritizes mental health, encourages open dialogue, and provides resources for lawyers to thrive both personally and professionally.

6.1 THE STRENGTH OF CONNECTION: CREATING A SUPPORTIVE NETWORK

Feeling connected and supported within the legal community is vital for the well-being of its members. Legal organizations can nurture these connections by:

a. Encouraging Peer Support Groups: Facilitating peer support groups gives lawyers a safe and understanding space to share their experiences and challenges. These groups become a valuable source of advice and empathy. The power of "mastermind" groups has been shown since 1727 when Benjamin Franklin created "The Junto Club" (also known as the Leather Apron Club). See Section 5.2.B.6 above.

b. Hosting Wellness Events: Organizing wellness events focused on mental health, stress reduction, and resilience-building can make a significant impact. Workshops, seminars, and webinars featuring mental health experts provide valuable insights and strategies.
c. Establishing Mentoring Programs: Mentorship programs pair experienced lawyers with junior associates, creating opportunities for personal and professional growth. Mentors offer guidance and support, fostering the development of their mentees.

6.2 CHALLENGING THE STIGMA: OPENING THE DIALOGUE ON MENTAL HEALTH

Breaking the culture of silence and stigma around mental health in the legal profession requires proactive steps:

a. Promote Mental Health Awareness: Organize events or campaigns during Mental Health Awareness Month or other relevant occasions to raise awareness. Make information and resources on mental health support readily available.
b. Offer Employee Assistance Programs (EAPs): Provide confidential support and counseling through EAPs for employees facing personal challenges, including mental health concerns. Encourage employees to utilize these resources without fear of judgment. See Section 6.7.
c. Train Leaders in Mental Health Support: Equip leaders and partners with the skills and knowledge to support their team members' mental well-being. Training should focus on recognizing signs of distress and providing appropriate assistance when needed. Let's create an environment where seeking help for mental health is encouraged and supported.

6.3 ADVOCATING FOR WORK–LIFE INTEGRATION: REDEFINING LEGAL WORKSPACES

Work–life integration, as opposed to work–life balance, acknowledges the interconnectivity of personal and professional aspects of life. Legal organizations can advocate for work–life integration by:

a. Implementing Flextime Policies: Offer flexible work arrangements that accommodate personal commitments without compromising productivity. Flextime policies demonstrate a commitment to work–life integration.
b. Encouraging Vacation and Time Off: Encourage lawyers to take time off regularly to recharge and rejuvenate. Avoid praising or promoting overworking as a sign of dedication.
c. Valuing Results Over Hours: Recognize and reward quality work and results rather than the number of hours worked. This shift in focus encourages efficiency and acknowledges the importance of downtime.

6.4 PROMOTING LEADERSHIP IN WELL-BEING

Leaders within legal organizations play a pivotal role in promoting well-being among their teams. Leadership can lead by example by:

a. Prioritizing Their Own Well-Being: Leaders should prioritize their mental health and demonstrate the importance of self-care through their actions.
b. Incorporating Well-Being into Organizational Goals: Embed well-being and resilience as core values in the organization's mission and vision.
c. Advocating for Change: Encourage discussions about mental health and well-being during team meetings and address challenges proactively.

6.5 A CALL FOR COLLABORATION: A COLLECTIVE RESPONSIBILITY

As we embark on the path toward a more supportive legal community, the responsibility lies with each one of us. Lawyers, law firms, legal associations, and governing bodies must come together to build an environment that places mental health at the forefront and nurtures a sense of mutual support.

Through embracing a culture that values well-being, we can conquer the obstacles presented by the mental health crisis, empowering one another to pursue fulfilling careers and lead lives enriched with purpose. Together, let's shape a legal profession that embodies compassion, resilience, and prosperity for every single member.

6.6 THE ABA PLEDGE AND EXPECTATIONS

The ABA and state bar associations have had committees supporting attorney well-being since the late 1970s. The ABA Hazleton study in 2016 was a wakeup call that attorney well-being was suffering and addiction levels were higher than previously recognized. More resources were dedicated to attorney sobriety and well-being with most states requiring mandatory well-being CLE. Unfortunately, the Massachusetts study has shown that the situation has gotten worse, not better, probably due to the COVID-19 crisis.

In 2017, the ABA formulated a pledge for legal employers to provide a safe and supportive working environment for legal personnel. For the employers that signed the pledge, it committed to the following components for a healthy workspace:

1. To provide enhanced and robust education for everyone in the workplace on well-being, mental health, and substance abuse.

2. To reduce the expectation of alcohol at events by creating creative alternatives.
3. Partner with outside providers who are committed to reducing substance abuse and mental health issues in the legal arena.
4. Provide confidential access to addiction to mental health experts and experts.
5. Develop proactive policies and protocols to support assessment and treatment of substance abuse and mental health issues.
6. Show that the workplace's core values include self-care and getting help.
7. Use the pledge to attract and retain the best individuals in the organization.

The ABA also published a lengthy *Well-Being Toolkit for Lawyers and Legal Employers.*[177] Hopefully the tips and suggestions in this book will go a long way to solving these problems.

6.7 A RADICAL IDEA

If we are going to get ahead of this crisis, we will have to do a better job of monitoring the mental health of practicing lawyers. Here are some practical but radical ways of getting not only attorneys but also family and others involved in the process.

A. Mentors

I have no idea of how many retired or "of counsel" lawyers exist in the world. To me, these lawyers are a largely untapped resource of support and maintenance for practicing lawyers. I would propose that any of these "seasoned" attorneys that want to serve can serve as monitors for practicing lawyers and hold regular (quarterly) meetings with every practicing lawyer in their district. They would get to know the lawyers and monitor their mental, emotional, and physical health. If this were mandatory, a lot of the stigma of talking to someone would be avoided.

B. Involve Family

We need to have all lawyers sign an agreement that we can talk to family or colleagues who are concerned about the lawyer. Oftentimes in a culture of silence, an agreement will find a trove of information that the lawyer has secreted. When we break through the culture of silence, we may save a lot of lawyers' mental and emotional health.

C. Involve Colleagues

I would think that as a collective, we need to start being more transparent about lawyers who are suffering and burning out. If the lawyer signs a waiver giving permission for people to report on their mental and emotional condition, it would go a long way to getting people help.

Conclusion: Thriving Together, A Journey of Resilience, Self-Care, and Support

The legal profession has grappled with burnout and mental health challenges, but a new narrative is taking charge—one that puts well-being, resilience, and community front and center. Throughout this journey, we've faced the harsh reality of burnout's impact and the pressing need to redefine success. Self-care is no longer a luxury; it's an absolute must for fortifying our mental strength and tackling challenges with unwavering grace.

The future demands that we prioritize our mental and emotional well-being, crafting a legal profession that exudes compassion and unwavering strength. The power to thrive rests within us, and we shall mold a brighter tomorrow for ourselves and our community.

Hand in hand, we strive toward a transformative era—a legal profession built on resilience and well-being—a journey of thriving together. With determination and relentless support, we shall conquer every challenge, emerging mightier than ever before.

Endnotes

1. https://www.norc.org/research/projects/massachusetts-lawyer-well-being-study.html
2. https://calawyers.org/california-lawyers-association/cla-and-d-c-bar-announce-more-findings-from-groundbreaking-study-on-attorney-mental-health-and-well-being/
3. https://www.abajournal.com/news/article/younger_lawyers_are_most_at_risk_for_substance_abuse_and_mental_health_prob
4. https://journals.lww.com/journaladdictionmedicine/fulltext/2016/02000/the_prevalence_of_substance_use_and_other_mental.8.aspx
5. For links to my articles, please visit https://www.jamesgrayrobinson.com.
6. https://www.psychiatry.org/patients-families/depression/what-is-depression
7. https://www.nimh.nih.gov/health/topics/depression
8. https://www.abajournal.com/news/article/mental-health-initiatives-arent-curbing-lawyer-stress-and-anxiety-new-study-shows
9. https://www.clio.com/blog/dealing-with-lawyer-depression/
10. https://www.bearing-academy.com/Why-do-people-want-to-become-lawyers-What-are-the-potential-benefits-of-becoming-a-lawyer#:~:text=Practicing%20law%20is%20financially%20and,law%20as%20a%20prestigious%20profession
11. https://bettertherapy.com/blog/depression-as-self-protection/
12. https://individual.carefirst.com/individuals-families/transformation/complete-care/how-bolster-mental-health-defenses.page
13. For a discussion of suicide among lawyers, see https://www.ncbi.nlm.nih.gov/pmc/articles/PMC9956925/#:~:text=Given%20the%20high%20rates%20of,10%2C11%2C12%5D.
14. For a discussion on the problem with compassion fatigue, see https://www.ncbi.nlm.nih.gov/pmc/articles/PMC7560777/).
15. *Id.*
16. For the ABA's look at stress, see https://www.americanbar.org/groups/lawyer_assistance/resources/stress/.
17. *Id.*

18. For a discussion of how parents affect their child's mental health, see https://integrisok.com/resources/on-your-health/2021/may/how-parents-affect-their-child-mental-health#:~:text=For%20example%2C%20parents%20who%20overprotect,lead%20to%20anxiety%20or%20depression.
19. For a discussion of how parental pressure often leads to increased stress and anxiety, see https://www.solhapp.com/blog/effects-of-parental-pressure-and-how-to-avoid-it#:~:text=In%20today's%20cutthroat%20competitive%20world,to%20increased%20stress%20and%20anxiety.
20. https://www.americanbar.org/groups/gpsolo/publications/gpsolo_ereport/2022/february-2022/legal-burnout-solution-how-improve-self-esteem/
21. https://www.goodtherapy.org/learn-about-therapy/issues/emotional-overwhelm
22. https://legal.thomsonreuters.com/blog/todays-lawyers-and-mental-health/
23. Abigail A. Patthoff, *This is Your Brain on Law School: The Impact of Fear-Based Narratives on Law Students*, 2015 Utah L. Rev. 391–424 (2015).
24. For a fascinating discussion of the dichotomy between the way law is decided and how lawyers think, see https://law.loyno.edu/sites/law.loyno.edu/files/images/07_55LoyLRev45(2009).pdf.
25. https://www.linkedin.com/pulse/escaping-perfectionism-trap-guide-lawyers-find-balance-gary-miles/
26. https://abovethelaw.com/career-files/how-people-pleasing-holds-lawyers-back/
27. https://lsj.com.au/articles/the-problem-with-perfection/
28. https://blog.lawline.com/attorneys-battle-imposter-syndrome-and-how-to-deal-with-it
29. See, https://psychcentral.com/lib/reasons-you-dont-listen.
30. https://positivepsychology.com/neuroplasticity/
31. https://mentalhealthhealingman.medium.com/the-real-reasons-why-lawyers-dont-seek-support-for-mental-health-a2da61289f23
32. For a discussion on eliminating stigma, see https://www.springhealth.com/blog/4-ways-address-mental-health-stigma-legal-community#:~:text=and%20need%20support.-,Many%20lawyers%20are%20afraid%20that%20asking%20for%20help%20could%20make,able%20to%20handle%20any%20challenge.
33. https://www.npr.org/2014/03/23/291405829/with-sobering-science-doctor-debunks-12-step-recovery
34. https://mentalhealthhealingman.medium.com/the-real-reasons-why-lawyers-dont-seek-support-for-mental-health-a2da61289f23

35. For a discussion on the origins of the statement "the law is a jealous mistress," see https://digitalcommons.du.edu/cgi/viewcontent.cgi?article=7083&context=dlr.
36. https://www.attorneysondemand.net/Sacrifice.cfm
37. https://jcf.org/mythblasts/sacrificial-origins/
38. https://thebestbrainpossible.com/mental-health-neuroplasticity-brain-habits-negative/
39. https://macleans.ca/society/lawyer-mental-health/
40. For a discussion on how lawyers can ask for help, see https://lawfirmsuites.com/2020/08/04/how-lawyers-should-ask-for-help-when-they-need-it-most/#:~:text=Lawyers%20respect%20competence%20in%20others,instead%20of%20asking%20for%20help.
41. For a discussion on understanding secondary trauma effect on lawyers, see https://www.americanbar.org/groups/public_interest/child_law/resources/child_law_practiceonline/child_law_practice/vol-34/september-2015/understanding-secondary-trauma--a-guide-for-lawyers-working-with/.
42. For a discussion on the problems of lawyer loneliness, see https://www.attorneyatwork.com/lawyer-loneliness/#:~:text=As%20reported%20recently%20in%20Harvard,stress%2C%20burnout%20and%20relationship%20turmoil.
43. https://medium.com/illumination/how-intelligence-and-smartness-trap-us-in-a-biased-mindset-aed762bcca80
44. https://www.psychologytoday.com/us/basics/unconscious
45. For a discussion on tests to uncover implicit bias, see https://implicit.harvard.edu/implicit/takeatest.html (Tests to uncover implicit bias).
46. *See generally,* https://www.ncbi.nlm.nih.gov/pmc/articles/PMC2762124/.
47. For a discussion on the interaction of stress and addiction, see https://www.ncbi.nlm.nih.gov/pmc/articles/PMC6308142/#:~:text=It%20is%20well%2Dknown%20that,for%20drug%20consumption%20and%20relapse.
48. https://wellnessretreatrecovery.com/alcohol-and-stress/
49. For a discussion on drink like a lawyer, the neuroscience of substance use and its impact on cognitive wellness, see https://scholars.law.unlv.edu/cgi/viewcontent.cgi?article=1598&context=nlj.
50. For a discussion on the effects of alcohol on the brain, see https://www.science.org/doi/10.1126/scitranslmed.3002902.
51. For a discussion on neuroscience of the brain on alcohol, see https://www.niaaa.nih.gov/health-professionals-communities/core-resource-on-alcohol/neuroscience-brain-addiction-and-recovery.
52. For a discussion on the effects of stress on drinking, see https://www.ncbi.nlm.nih.gov/pmc/articles/PMC5497303/.

53. For a discussion on women and alcohol, see https://www.niaaa.nih.gov/publications/brochures-and-fact-sheets/women-and-alcohol#:~:text=There%20is%20an%20association%20between,do%20not%20drink%20at%20all.&text=That%20risk%20increases%20for%20every%20additional%20drink%20they%20have%20per%20day.
54. For a discussion on the effects of alcohol on health, see https://www.cdc.gov/alcohol/fact-sheets/alcohol-use.htm#:~:text=Over%20time%2C%20excessive%20alcohol%20use,liver%20disease%2C%20and%20digestive%20problems.
55. For a discussion on the anatomy of the ANS, see https://www.ncbi.nlm.nih.gov/books/NBK539845/#:~:text=Introduction,sympathetic%2C%20parasympathetic%2C%20and%20enteric.
56. https://www.health.harvard.edu/staying-healthy/understanding-the-stress-response
57. https://www.medicinenet.com/symptoms_of_an_overactive_nervous_system/article.htm
58. https://www.gabekwakyi.com/essays/work-burnout-symptoms
59. For a discussion on the physiology of the ANS, see https://www.ncbi.nlm.nih.gov/pmc/articles/PMC1959222/#:~:text=The%20sympathetic%20system%20controls%20%E2%80%9Cfight,%E2%80%9Crest%20and%20digest%E2%80%9D%20functions.
60. https://psychcentral.com/blog/you-are-not-your-thoughts#1
61. https://www.bloomberglaw.com/external/document/XA4SG9K4000000/litigation-professional-perspective-building-resilience-in-the-l
62. https://hbr.org/2021/01/what-you-were-taught-about-happiness-isnt-true
63. For a discussion on the difference between happy and unhappy people, see https://www.ncbi.nlm.nih.gov/pmc/articles/PMC4771683/.
64. https://www.huffpost.com/entry/what-is-a-hero_b_5560441
65. https://www.psychologytoday.com/us/blog/anxiety-zen/201511/why-is-happiness-so-hard-10-reasons-10-solutions
66. https://amymorinlcsw.com/youre-a-product-of-your-choices-not-a-victim-of-your-circumstances/
67. https://www.psychologytoday.com/us/blog/how-be-yourself/202011/6-ways-not-take-things-personally
68. https://www.mayoclinic.org/tests-procedures/resilience-training/in-depth/resilience/art-20046311
69. https://poets.org/poem/hamlet-act-iii-scene-i-be-or-not-be
70. For a discussion on the effects of COVID-19 on mental health, see https://www.sciencedirect.com/science/article/pii/S0924977X21016357.
71. https://dictionary.cambridge.org/us/dictionary/english/resilience

72. For a discussion on the explanation of mastermind groups, see https://www.naphill.org/focus-instructors/mastermind/.
73. https://www.abajournal.com/voice/article/how-lawyers-can-build-resilience
74. https://health.clevelandclinic.org/what-happens-when-your-immune-system-gets-stressed-out
75. For a discussion on laughter reducing stress and raising self-esteem, see https://www.mayoclinic.org/healthy-lifestyle/stress-management/in-depth/stress-relief/art-20044456#:~:text=Laughter%20can%20help%20lessen%20your,also%20improve%20your%20self%2Desteem.
76. For a discussion on our choices whether something is a miracle or disaster, see https://www.taosnews.com/opinion/columns/miracle-or-disaster-its-a-matter-of-choice/article_b30cc59a-7cf1-5be0-afca-c16e421d4ac0.html.
77. For a discussion on desire and ignorance being the source of all suffering, see https://www.pbs.org/edens/thailand/buddhism.htm#:~:text=In%20Buddhism%2C%20desire%20and%20ignorance,them%20can%20only%20bring%20suffering.
78. https://clp.law.harvard.edu/knowledge-hub/magazine/issues/approaching-lawyer-well-being/capitalizing-on-healthy-lawyers/
79. https://www.americanbar.org/groups/public_interest/child_law/resources/child_law_practiceonline/child_law_practice/vol-34/september-2015/understanding-secondary-trauma–a-guide-for-lawyers-working-with/
80. https://counseling.northwestern.edu/blog/self-care-strategies-for-managing-secondary-traumatic-stress/
81. For a discussion on taking breaks being critical to optimal performance, see https://www.forbes.com/sites/alankohll/2018/05/29/new-study-shows-correlation-between-employee-engagement-and-the-long-lost-lunch-break/?sh=4cdf5fa34efc..
82. For a discussion on trauma and PTSD, see https://www.ncbi.nlm.nih.gov/pmc/articles/PMC3182008/.
83. https://harbormentalhealth.com/2023/04/03/how-to-deal-with-negative-self-talk/
84. For a discussion on gratitude being the answer to anxiety, see http://www.tntechoracle.com/2022/11/08/is-gratitude-the-answer-to-anxiety/#:~:text=However%2C%20the%20most%20profound%20thing,feel%20anxious%20is%20practicing%20gratitude.
85. https://americanbehavioralclinics.com/10-signs-of-emotional-maturity/
86. https://www.scientificamerican.com/article/persuasion-fatigue-is-a-unique-form-of-social-frustration/
87. https://www.therapynowsf.com/blog/mind-reading-the-problems-it-can-cause

88. https://www.abajournal.com/voice/article/mindfulness-and-spirituality-for-lawyers
89. For a discussion on if lawyers should defend human dignity and not assault it, see https://scholarship.law.georgetown.edu/cgi/viewcontent.cgi?article=1164&context=facpub.
90. For a discussion on how your thinking creates your reality, see https://www.psychologytoday.com/us/blog/living-forward/202009/how-your-thinking-creates-your-reality#:~:text=You%20write%20the%20story%20of,participate%20in%20creating%20the%20experience.
91. For a discussion on what projection is, see https://www.psychologytoday.com/us/basics/projection.
92. For a discussion on coping with setbacks through letting go, see https://www.psychologytoday.com/us/blog/flex-your-feelings/202209/the-importance-letting-go.
93. https://www.nih.gov/news-events/nih-research-matters/healthy-habits-can-lengthen-life
94. For a discussion on the importance of compassion and empathy in lawyers, see https://web.law.duke.edu/sites/default/files/clinics/healthjustice/gerdy_-_the_heart_of_lawyering_clients_empathy_and_compassion.pdf.
95. https://positivepsychology.com/why-is-compassion-important/
96. https://www.psychologytoday.com/us/blog/in-flux/201510/when-the-best-you-can-be-is-not-good-enough
97. For a discussion on the difference between shame and disgust and their effects on the mind, see https://www.ncbi.nlm.nih.gov/pmc/articles/PMC7040959/#:~:text=The%20experience%20of%20shame%20encourages,is%20perceived%20as%20innately%20flawed.
98. For a discussion on shame, see https://www.choosingtherapy.com/shame/#:~:text=Shame%20describes%20feelings%20of%20inadequacy,self%2Dcritical%2C%20and%20embarrassed.
99. https://online.hbs.edu/blog/post/emotional-intelligence-in-leadership
100. For a discussion on emotional intelligence as a predictor for success, see https://www.ncbi.nlm.nih.gov/pmc/articles/PMC1636947/.
101. For a discussion on emotional intelligence being twice as important as intellectual skills, see https://www.wartsila.com/insights/article/why-eq-is-more-important-than-iq#:~:text=Dr%20Bradley%20explains%2C%20%E2%80%9CEQ%20is,comes%20to%20effectiveness%20at%20work.%E2%80%9D.
102. https://hbr.org/2018/01/what-self-awareness-really-is-and-how-to-cultivate-it
103. https://www.forbes.com/sites/petekrasspiersonkrass/2018/08/23/do-you-learn-more-from-failure-or-success/?sh=76c0b78f57de

104. https://hbr.org/2011/04/strategies-for-learning-from-failure
105. https://www.theladders.com/career-advice/new-study-shows-we-learn-less-from-failure-than-success
106. https://www.abajournal.com/voice/article/how-attorneys-can-claim-their-power
107. https://www.trcp.org/2011/01/18/it-is-not-the-critic-who-counts/
108. https://emotional-intelligence-training.weebly.com/arrested-emotional-development.html
109. https://www.webmd.com/mental-health/what-is-a-emotional-immaturity
110. For a discussion on Erickson's stages of psychosocial development, see https://www.ncbi.nlm.nih.gov/books/NBK556096/.
111. For a discussion on stages of emotional development, see https://www.ncbi.nlm.nih.gov/books/NBK534819/.
112. For a discussion on why we need to control emotions, see https://my.clevelandclinic.org/health/symptoms/25065-emotional-dysregulation.
113. For a discussion on what emotional maturity is, see https://www.healthline.com/health/mental-health/emotional-maturity#:~:text=Taking%20responsibility,yourself)%20when%20something%20goes%20awry.
114. https://www.hphi.life/hphi-blog/how-to-accomplish-your-life-goals-the-power-of-frequent-course-correction
115. https://www.researchgate.net/publication/333918011_Emotional_Maturity_and_Happiness_among_Emerging_Adults
116. https://psychcentral.com/blog/self-care-why-is-it-so-important-why-is-it-so-hard#1
117. https://tinybuddha.com/blog/love-relationships-blog/what-to-do-when-you-cant-seem-to-love-yourself/
118. https://sweetinstitute.com/conscious-unconscious-alignment/
119. https://www.lifeoptimizer.org/2016/08/02/subconscious-negativity/
120. https://positivepsychology.com/benefits-motivation/
121. https://addicted2success.com/motivation/positive-motivation-vs-negative-motivation-which-one-works-better/
122. https://www.abajournal.com/voice/article/how-lawyers-can-strengthen-their-minds-by-identifying-and-overcoming-implicit-bias
123. https://www.ceotodaymagazine.com/2022/06/why-self-acceptance-is-the-key-to-success/
124. For a discussion on the spiritual significance of the law, see https://scholarship.law.stjohns.edu/cgi/viewcontent.cgi?article=1244&context=tcl#:~:text=The%20spirit%20of%20justice%20is,sig%2D%20nificance%20of%20their%20calling.

125. https://abovethelaw.com/career-files/why-lawyers-need-to-pay-attention-to-spirituality/
126. For a discussion on why spirituality matters to lawyers, see https://academic.oup.com/ojlr/article-abstract/8/2/326/5531251.
127. https://newsinhealth.nih.gov/2012/01/mindfulness-matters
128. For a discussion on the explanation of polyvagal theory, see https://www.ncbi.nlm.nih.gov/pmc/articles/PMC3108032/#:~:text=The%20polyvagal%20theory%20proposes%20that,of%20behavior%20and%20psychological%20experience.
129. For a discussion on the physiology of the brain, see https://www.ncbi.nlm.nih.gov/pmc/articles/PMC1959222/.
130. For a discussion on the physiology of the brain, see https://www.ncbi.nlm.nih.gov/pmc/articles/PMC1959222/.
131. For a discussion on the evolution of the brain, see https://www.frontiersin.org/articles/10.3389/fnana.2011.00029/full.
132. https://www.webmd.com/brain/parasympathetic-nervous-system-what-to-know
133. For a discussion on how the ANS affects how we see, see https://www.frontiersin.org/articles/10.3389/fncom.2023.1136985/full.
134. https://www.med.umich.edu/1libr/PedPsych/AutonomicNervousSystemHowToControl.pdf
135. https://ct.counseling.org/2016/06/polyvagal-theory-practice/
136. For a discussion on the functions of the ANS and PNS, see https://www.ncbi.nlm.nih.gov/pmc/articles/PMC7117974/.
137. For a discussion on the chronic activation of the SNS causing higher cognitive decline while longer PNS activity supports cognitive maintenance, see https://www.ncbi.nlm.nih.gov/pmc/articles/PMC7117974/.
138. https://www.health.harvard.edu/staying-healthy/understanding-the-stress-response
139. https://www.ncbi.nlm.nih.gov/books/NBK553141/#article-26653.s1 (neuroanatomy of PNS).
140. https://www.simplypsychology.org/maslow.html
141. https://re-origin.com/articles/neuroplasticity-and-positive-thinking/
142. Dr. Joe Vitale & Dr. Ihaleakala Hew Len, PhD, Zero Limits, (John Wiley & Sons, Inc.) (2007).
143. For a discussion on the advantages of Ho'oponopono meditation, see https://www2.hawaii.edu/~barkai/HO/Hooponopono.pdf.
144. https://www.lauraferrerphd.com/insights/hooponopono-meditation-for-healing

145. https://ct.counseling.org/2016/06/polyvagal-theory-practice/
146. https://www.allied-services.org/news/2020/june/the-vagus-nerve-your-secret-weapon-in-fighting-s/#:~:text=Loud%20gargling%20with%20water%20or,both%20cheeks%20into%20cold%20water.
147. https://www.publish0x.com/antonmakarski/hakalau-the-ancient-hawaiian-meditation-peripheral-vision-xdnvlxx
148. https://www.healthline.com/health/mantra-meditation#mantras
149. https://re-origin.com/articles/neuroplasticity-and-positive-thinking/
150. For a discussion on hypothyroidism contributing to higher cortisol levels, see https://www.ncbi.nlm.nih.gov/pmc/articles/PMC3520819/.
151. For a discussion on stress negatively impacting health and well-being, see https://www.apa.org/topics/stress/health.
152. https://www.mayoclinic.org/diseases-conditions/depression/in-depth/depression-and-exercise/art-20046495
153. For a discussion on how exercise reduces stress, see https://www.health.harvard.edu/staying-healthy/exercising-to-relax#:~:text=The%20mental%20benefits%20of%20aerobic,natural%20painkillers%20and%20mood%20elevators.
154. https://www.health.harvard.edu/blog/nutritional-psychiatry-your-brain-on-food-201511168626
155. https://www.apa.org/monitor/2023/06/nutrition-for-mental-health-depression
156. https://www.floridabar.org/the-florida-bar-news/be-a-healthy-lawyer/
157. https://www.nytimes.com/2019/08/26/opinion/food-nutrition-health-care.html
158. For a discussion on hugging reducing cortisol, increasing oxycontin, and lowering blood pressure, see https://www.ncbi.nlm.nih.gov/pmc/articles/PMC3805974/.
159. For a discussion on communication and contact having positive physiological benefits, see https://www.psychcaremd.com/hardwired-for-connection/.
160. https://www.psychologytoday.com/us/blog/in-it-together/201809/the-neuroscience-feeling-safe-and-connected
161. For a discussion on solitary confinement increasing the risk of death, see https://www.nami.org/Blogs/NAMI-Blog/March-2023/How-Solitary-Confinement-Contributes-to-the-Mental-Health-Crisis.
162. For an interview with the owner of several mastermind groups made up of law firm owners, see https://www.forbes.com/sites/rodberger/2023/01/06/mastermind-groups-approach-education-through-alternative-learning-models/?sh=1d9e86936d75.

163. For a discussion on war and the Vanishing Battlefield and how the law has affected battle, see https://lawecommons.luc.edu/cgi/viewcontent.cgi?article=1013&context=lucilr.
164. For a discussion on overlooked functions of conflict litigation by international courts, see https://scholarship.law.duke.edu/cgi/viewcontent.cgi?article=5022&context=lcp.
165. For a discussion on applying five universal human values to medicine, see https://www.scirp.org/journal/paperinformation?paperid=99676.
166. https://thepeakperformancecenter.com/development-series/skill-builder/personal-effectiveness/goal-setting/benefits-of-goal-setting/
167. https://thepeakperformancecenter.com/development-series/skill-builder/personal-effectiveness/goal-setting/benefits-of-goal-setting/
168. NAPOLEAN HILL, THINK AND GROW RICH (Chump Change Publishing, 1937).
169. For a discussion on being a Buddhist and a lawyer, see https://ir.lawnet.fordham.edu/cgi/viewcontent.cgi?article=3428&context=flr.
170. For a discussion on the key to changing your life being mind control, see https://www.todayswomannow.com/mind-control-the-new-frontier-of-the-mind-body-connection/#:~:text=The%20term%20%E2%80%9Cmind%20control,%2C%20%E2%80%9CThe%20mind%20is%20everything.
171. https://www.americanbar.org/news/abanews/publications/youraba/2017/april-2017/using-the-practice-of-mindfulness-to-improve-your-law-practice-/
172. https://www.aliesq.com/articles/2012/8/28/buddhism-and-the-practice-of-law
173. For a discussion on the Four Noble Truths, see https://www.pbs.org/edens/thailand/buddhism.htm#:~:text=The%20Four%20Noble%20Truths&text=They%20are%20the%20truth%20of,to%20bring%20about%20its%20end.
174. For a discussion on the history, philosophy, and practice of Buddhism, see https://buddha101.com/p_path.htm.
175. https://news.gallup.com/poll/1654/honesty-ethics-professions.aspx
176. For a discussion on observing the hidden aspects of ourselves in the actions and behaviors of those we observe, see https://www.thesap.org.uk/articles-on-jungian-psychology-2/about-analysis-and-therapy/the-shadow/.
177. https://www.americanbar.org/content/dam/aba/administrative/lawyer_assistance/ls_colap_well-being_toolkit_for_lawyers_legal_employers.pdf

Appendix

Affirmations

Affirmations are one of the oldest ways to train your mind to think positively and properly. Many ancient cultures use mantras and affirmations to magically create energy fields that foster positive change in themselves and thereby the world. These affirmations and mantras can change your perception, your attitude, and your reality. I have listed 52 affirmation examples which can be repeated daily for one week each. This would give you one year of affirmations to form a new habitual way of thinking. You can modify, add, substitute, amend these, or change the order as you see fit. The important thing, like forming any new habit, is repetition.

1. **I can achieve greatness.** One of the most influential ones is to tell yourself on a daily basis that you can achieve all the greatness in life. Focus on your vision and dreams and then attach the emotion to that vision. By telling this to yourself and believing that you can achieve greatness, it will eventually turn into reality.
2. **Today, I am brimming with energy and overflowing with joy.** Joy starts from within, not from outside of, yourself. It also starts as soon as you rise. So, make it a habit to repeat this to yourself first thing in the morning.
3. **I love and accept myself for who I am.** Self-love is meant to be the purest and the highest form of love. When you love yourself, you automatically start appreciating and

respecting yourself. If you have confidence and pride in what you do, you will begin to see yourself in a new light and be encouraged and inspired to do bigger and better things.

4. **My body is healthy, my mind is brilliant, my soul is tranquil.** A healthy body starts with a healthy mind and soul. If either suffers from negative emotions, the others will be affected. You can also remove and revoke all permission that you have given consciously, subconsciously, to all the ills of the world because you share that pain. You are conquering your illness and defeating it steadily each day.
5. **I believe I can do everything.** You need to say this to yourself every day. Because this is something that is so important for counselling yourself to stay encouraged. By saying this, you are able to do anything and everything that you put your mind to.
6. **Everything that is happening now is happening for my ultimate good.** There are no victims, no accidents, and no coincidences EVER. They simply do not exist in this reality as you and others will only attract what you and they are a part of. So, know from the bottom of your heart that everything happens for a reason and in perfect synchronicity. You are at peace with all that has happened, is happening, and will happen. Your fears of tomorrow are simply melting away.
7. **I am the architect of my life; I build its foundation and choose its contents.**This is something that you should tell yourself when you wake up every morning. Every new day offers a fresh start and also makes an impact on others around you. You can make anything of that day that you like because you are the architect of your own life. If you begin your day with a positive thought

and feeling it will transform your day into something incredible. Works every time.

8. **I forgive those who have harmed me in my past and peacefully detach from them.** That doesn't mean you forget what they did, but you are at peace with what they did, and the lessons served. Your strength to forgive is what allows you to move forward and your reaction to any experience is independent of what others think of you. You can forgive one thousand people and even if none of them forgive you, there will always be a sense of peace and freedom within you that they will never have until they share that sentiment. Your power to forgive them also instantly changes how they react to you.
9. **I forgive myself and release my negative opinions of myself.** Forgiving yourself is the first step to achieve a state of grace. It is necessary to achieve any equanimity or peace in our life. It is the acceptance that we are human and don't always behave or think as we in hindsight might wish. It is to accept ourselves for who we are.
10. **My ability to conquer my challenges is limitless; my potential to succeed is infinite.** Plain and simple, you have no limits but those you place on yourself. What kind of life do you want? What is stopping you? What barriers are you imposing on yourself? This affirmation will help you address all of the boundaries.
11. **Today, I abandon my old habits and take up new, more positive ones.** Realize that any difficult time is only a short phase of life. This too shall pass along with your old habits as you take in the new. You are a fully adapting being with creative energy which surges through you and leads you to new and brilliant ideas and the mindset that allows that energy to flow.

12. **My subconscious is free from fear and is a loving foundation for my life.** Our subconscious mind is the source of all our emotions and feelings. When we instruct it to be fearless and supportive, it will obey. The theory is that our thoughts create our reality, so we must properly program the operating system (subconscious) to create a positive reality.
13. **I am happy and grateful to be alive and for every gift my god has given me.** Whatever we focus on expands. If we focus on happiness and gratitude, our subconscious mind will obey those thoughts and give you reasons to be happy and grateful.
14. **Every day in every way I am getting better and better.** This is the affirmation of hope and trust. When we repeat this affirmation, we create the space into which we can grow. When we are thinking negative thoughts such as "I am unworthy" or "I am a failure," there is no room to grow. This affirmation creates the space we need to grow.
15. **I am not my thoughts and I let go of any thoughts that cause me suffering.** It is important to remember that we are not our minds. Our minds are just a tool to help us in this 3D reality. Our higher aspects are connected to the divine who directs and controls our reality. Due to trauma and fear, our minds get out of control and spiral down into worst-case scenario thinking that is adopted by our subconscious and it becomes our reality. This affirmation helps to detach from our thoughts so we can experience our divine connection.
16. **I am filled with faith, trust, confidence, and certainty.** This affirmation replaces the older, fear-based beliefs and emotions that may be lurking in our subconscious. When we know that we are following the divine plan,

we will feel confident and sure. This creates thoughts of a similar nature and raises our vibration to the level of positive manifestation.

17. **Just for today I will . . .** Sometimes our fears and our troubled mind are overwhelmed. When we set a specific time, we will think, feel, or believe in a certain way. It is easier to take it one step at a time. Instead of open-ended affirmations, we can take bite-sized periods that our minds can accept. We can direct our subconscious mind and our behavior in any direction for one day, one hour, one minute. In this way, we slowly and surely change our reality.
18. **I am filled with joy, light, and excitement.** Some people are afraid to let their light shine. When we are filled with joy, our light expands and fills any space we occupy. When we are excited, we pass that excitement on to others. When we affirm that consciousness and begin to reprogram our subconscious mind with these concepts, there is a difference in our demeanor, attitude, and behavior. We will infect others with these energies and our reality will become rewarding and fulfilling.
19. **My subconscious mind only transmits thoughts of love, confidence, and power to others.** This affirmation recognizes that we are in constant subconscious communication with all other beings on the planet. When we instruct our subconscious mind to act and think in a certain way, it will do so. When we are constantly broadcasting these higher thoughts and feelings to the world, those at similar frequencies will respond.
20. **I deserve all the love, abundance, and joy the universe has to offer (or better).** Sometimes we block our divine inheritance as children of the universe because we don't believe we deserve it. When we reprogram our

subconscious mind to start broadcasting to the universe that we deserve it, the universe will respond. We don't have to know where it will come from or when it will arrive. Our job is to declare that we deserve it and trust that the universe will deliver. The "or better" allows for the possibility that our minds are limited in scope and if the universe has something else planned which is better, we will accept that as well.

21. **May I, and all the beings in all the worlds, be happy.** Sometimes the simplest affirmations are the best. This creates a bubble of energy around each being and gives them the space to be happy. It requires us to let go of resentment, anger, and fear because you can't wish someone to be happy and be afraid of them at the same time. "I am happy" is one of the most powerful affirmations because it combines the creative sound of "I AM" (OM) and the state to which we all desire. When we wish happiness for others, we increase our capacity to be happy.
22. **I am . . .** Whatever you want to become, you have to believe you are. In order to create that belief, we say "I AM." So, if you want to create abundance, the affirmation is "I AM abundant." If you want to feel loved, say "I AM loved." The applications of this affirmation are unlimited.
23. **I am a beautiful being of light which shines throughout the universe. I am manifesting my dreams, and no dream is too big.** As human beings, we often are trained to dream small. When we accept our power, our HUGENESS, we tap into divine will, divine power, and divine opportunity. Dream BIG.
24. **Everything is in my own best interest.** How we perceive the world is an indication of the biases we harbour in our conscious and unconscious minds. When we repeat

a thought over and over it becomes a belief, and we start to see the synchronicities in the world and how they are conspiring to support us. If we believe everything happens for us, not to us, we feel more in control and can relax.

25. **I am more than this physical body.** We are actually multi-dimensional creations who are living in multiple realities, all at the same time. The reality we experience is the one we project onto the environment around us. When we understand we can create our own reality, we become more than a physical body.
26. **My thoughts create my life.** One of life's great ironies is that even though we are more than our thoughts, if we are attached to our beliefs and thoughts, that is the reality we will create. When we allow our thoughts to inspire us and motivate us for good, we can create the life we want.
27. **I can always control my thoughts.** When we start to notice our thoughts, we begin to understand that we can only think one thought at a time, and it is our choice which thought to think. When we remind ourselves that we don't have to let negative thoughts dominate our mental landscape, we can start looking at the positive nature of life and be in control.
28. **I am responsible for the way I see things.** The only way we can change is if we acknowledge we have the power to change. When we take responsibility for our reality, we begin to become accountable to ourselves for what life we live.
29. **I am entitled to miracles.** Some people don't believe in miracles, which is a shame because it limits the life they could have. If we think that we have to work hard for everything, that is the reality we experience. If we

believe in miracles, we can see the miracles that happen all around us, every day. The basic definition of a miracle is an extraordinary event which is unexplainable. We either see them or we don't, depending on whether we are looking and paying attention. Remind yourself that they exist, and you deserve to have them happen to you.

30. **I have the strength to feel my feelings.** Many people suppress their emotions because they don't want to deal with them, especially negative emotions. If we don't want to bury our negative emotions into our subconscious, where they will control our lives without our awareness of them, we will suffer. When we are strong enough to process them and learn their lessons, life becomes effortless.
31. **There is power in vulnerability.** Some people don't want to be vulnerable because they equate that with weakness. Actually, being vulnerable allows us to be authentic and connect with other human beings. When we embrace the negative emotions that complicate our lives, we can grow and become better people. By being vulnerable and connecting with other people, we can learn, expand our experience, and be more fulfilled.
32. **Fear is a prayer to God for love.** Contrary to popular belief, God does not need our thanks or praise. God wants our fear, our hate, our anger, and our shame so that He can transmute those negative emotions into love. When we are afraid, give that fear to God in prayer and feel the love fill the hole that your fear vacated.
33. **I have a purpose.** People seem to function better when they feel they have a purpose, and their goals are in alignment with that purpose. The only purpose of life is to experience it. Enjoy it and keep breathing. Our egos get in the way sometime and demand that we know

what that purpose is. We overthink, worry, and pole vault over mouse turds. When we keep it simple and accept life as the wonderful adventure it can be, we open ourselves to life's infinite abundance.

34. **I constantly expand and try new things.** We are either growing or dying. By definition, growth involves expansion and learning new ideas, concepts, behavior, and lessons. When we confirm that we are expanding and open to new aspects of life, we are confirming that we are alive. Learn something new every day and expand your consciousness.
35. **I choose to be excited.** There is a fine line between fear and excitement. We can choose whether we are afraid or excited. I find that positive people look forward to the future because they are excited about what they will find. Negative people are afraid of the future because they expect to have negative results. We choose whether we are positive or negative.
36. **I deserve to feel loved.** The first step to self-love is the belief that you deserve it. If you believe you are lovable, you can begin to love yourself which is critical to feeling loved. If you don't believe you are lovable, you will suffer. Affirm to the universe and yourself that you deserve love and to feel loved.
37. **Everyone I meet is a reflection of me.** There is a saying in psychology that "all perception is projection," or more accurately, "I see what I want to see." When we can acknowledge that everyone reflects my qualities, good and bad, then we can see ourselves in others. If we see someone we don't like, it is because there is a part of us that needs to be healed.
38. **I am always a teacher to someone.** Some people are teachers of how to be, others are teachers of how not to

be. We consciously or unconsciously choose which one we are going to be. When we are aware of this, we can make better decisions about how to behave.

39. **I trust everything is helping me be better.** Trust is the reliance on the truth, character, or abilities of someone or something. When we place our trust in ourselves, we can start to believe that the universe is conspiring about our success. Sometimes we get confused or rattled, but trust will carry us through.
40. **I am enough.** Probably one of the most debilitating beliefs we burden ourselves with is "I am not enough." It saps us of our strength and disconnects us from our divinity and spirituality. Many times, we come to that conclusion because we aren't getting what we want (which is a misconception that the quality of life is measured by what we own). The quality of our inner world determines the quality of our outer world.
41. **I am full of peace.** To be able to be in a state of grace allows us to experience life as we are designed to be. Not only do we have to be in a peaceful environment, but we also have to achieve mental equanimity and calmness. Enlightenment is simply the elimination of conflict in our lives, thoughts, and behavior.
42. **I am worthy and valuable.** It is a truth of human nature that the only person that can give us a sense of worth and value is ourselves. If we don't believe that, no one can convince us otherwise. When you repeat a thought often enough, it becomes a belief, which becomes behavior, which creates your life.
43. **I define my success, and I am successful.** What is your definition of success? Many people think of success by material standards: money, possessions, achievements. We determine what our definition of success is and judge

ourselves using that definition. Make sure your definition recognizes your inherent value.

44. **I am love.** Love is not something we do; it is something we are. When we think thoughts of love frequently enough, we begin to project that into the world. When we project that into the world, we begin to see it in people who are mirrors of us. When we recognize the love within us, we begin to be our authentic selves.
45. **I can do anything.** The only thing that limits our potential is our beliefs. If we believe we can do anything, we create the possibility of unlimited potential. When we release any negative thoughts, beliefs, or judgment, we open the door of opportunity. We are such powerful beings that we can achieve anything we believe.
46. **Let (inhale) go (exhale).** The ability to relax is critical for wellness. When we are stressed, tense, or upset, we must focus on releasing anything and everything that is causing that reaction in our mind and body. When we combine the thought of relaxing with our breath, we combine our physical, mental, and emotional minds to achieve peace within us.
47. **I decide how I feel.** Most people don't realize that we can control how we feel and allow their emotions to control their lives. In fact, it is the contrary, our thoughts can determine how we feel, and we have a choice. We can decide to feel excited rather than fear, we can feel valuable rather than worthless, we can feel successful rather than a failure.
48. **WOW!** Wow is one of those magical words that can disconnect (dissociate) us from what we are experiencing. When we experience negative emotions, simply say "wow!" and we can allow ourselves the grace to decide to feel differently.

49. **I am excited about the future.** We can get paralyzed by fear of the future and the unknown. We limit ourselves by choosing what we know even if it is uncomfortable over the unknown. What we don't realize is that the emotions of fear and excitement are very similar, separated only by the thin veil of choice. Rather than be afraid of something, get excited about it!
50. **Everything changes.** We often forget that nothing lasts forever. When we are feeling fear or shame it seems like we will be that way forever. In fact, everything changes whether we want it to or not. Consider how short life is and we should enjoy it as many minutes as possible. We are so powerful we can suffer, or we can celebrate whenever we want.
51. **Altitude is attitude.** What we can achieve and what we can accomplish depends significantly on how we think and feel about what we are doing. Our attitude about our work will directly affect how far we go in our careers. The most successful professionals are the ones that have a positive attitude about what they do. We have complete control over our attitude.
52. **I am perfect.** Many people get stressed over the fact that they think that they are failures or imperfect. We are human, and life is a lesson. We are not going to get everything we want nor are we going to avoid conflict. Conflict can be the spice of life or it can poison everything. It is our choice of how we perceive our life and our world. Everything we do is designed to help us grow mentally, emotionally, and spiritually. By having experiences and learning from them we are perfect.

Index

A
ABA Journal, 4, 53
Addiction, 41–42. *See also* Alcohol
Adrenaline, 33, 45
Alcohol, 41–42
  effects on the body, 43–44
  effects on the brain, 42–43
ALM Mental Health Survey of the Legal Profession, 7
"Always-on" culture, 25–27
American Bar Association (ABA), 3, 4, 34, 136–137
Anxiety, 5–10, 57, 86
  perfectionism and, 18
Attachment, 130
Autonomic nervous system (ANS), 45–47, 95–99
Awareness, 70

B
Behavior *versus* motivation, 89–90
Being your best, 76–82
Biases, 37–40
Blame, 18
Blue dot meditation, 106–107
Body, alcohol effects on, 43–44
Body scan meditation, 106
Boundaries, 11, 94–95
Box breathing, 105
Brain
  alcohol effects on, 42–43
  ANS and PNS and, 45–47, 95–96
Breaks, taking, 58
Breathing meditations, 105–106, 126
Buddha, 58, 116–120, 125
Burnout
  "always-on" culture and, 25–27
  character traits that can lead to, 10
  compassion fatigue *versus*, 11
  as epidemic, 3–5
  overactive SNS and, 46
  symptoms of, 83–84

C
Closed-mindedness, 18
Cognitive bias, 90
Cold water and vagus nerve, 104
Collaboration, 136
Colleagues, involvement of, 138
Common good, 50
Compassion, 8, 61

Compassion fatigue, 11, 60–61
Confidence, 72, 76–77, 91
Connections, 63, 110
Conscious mind, 88–92
Continuing legal education (CLE) requirements, 4
Control, feeling in, 76
Cooling breath, 106
Cortisol, 33, 45, 97
COVID-19 pandemic, 4, 34–36, 56, 72

D

Defensiveness, 18
Depression, 5–10, 86
  defined as mood disorder, 6
  prevalence of, 6–7
  reasons for lawyer susceptibility to, 8–9
  symptoms of, 7
Disclosure, fear of, 32
Disconnecting from emotion, 68

E

Emotional control, 68
Emotional intelligence, 69–82
Emotional maturity, 59, 79, 80–81
Empathy, 71
Employee Assistance Programs (EAPs), 134
Excellence/perfectionism, 8, 16–21
Exercise, 108–109

F

Facial nerves, 103
Faith. *See* spirituality
Family involvement, 138
Fears
  of perceived judgment, 31–33
  of perceived weakness, 23–25
  of professional consequences, 27–29
Feeding the soul, 58
Fight, flight or freeze response, 45, 96, 129
Flextime, 135
Focusing on one's own path, 60
Focusing on the positive, 57–58
Forgiveness, 101–102
Franklin, Benjamin, 133
Fun, 57

G

Goals and plans, 74, 114–116
Gratitude, 71–72, 102
Grit, 63–65
Guru mode, 45–48, 86, 95–99
  vagus nerve and, 103–104

H

Ha breath, 106
Hakalau, 104
Happiness, 49–51, 93–94
  resilience and, 56
Hazelton Betty Ford Foundation, 3
Health, physical, 108–109
Healthy habits, 62
Heroes, 50–52, 63
Hew Len, Ihaleakala, 100–101
High-pressure environments, 15–16
Hill, Napoleon, 57
Hobbies, 62
Honesty, 74
Ho'oponopono, 100–103, 107

Humming and vagus nerve, 104
Humming breath, 106
Humor, 63
Hurt feelings, 59

I
Identity, creating an, 73–74
Immune system and stress, 57
Implicit Association Test (IAT), 38–40
Implicit bias, 37–40
Imposter syndrome, 2, 9, 18–21, 77–78
 fear of perceived weakness and, 23–25
Inner dialogue, 67
Integrity, 61

J
Joy, 63
Judgment, 61, 128–129

K
Keith, Kent, 101
Kindness, 60–61

L
Lack of education and awareness, 34–35
Laughing, 63
Lawyers Assisting Lawyers (LAL), 21, 28
Lawyer well-being, 1–3
 anxiety and depression and, 5–10
 burnout epidemic and, 3–5
 in high-pressure environment, 15–16
 involving colleagues in, 138
 involving family in, 138
 mentors and, 137–138
 promoting leadership in, 135
 suicidal thoughts and, 10–11
Leadership training in mental health support, 134
Legal community, the
 call for collaboration in, 136
 creating a supportive network in, 133–134
 opening the dialogue on mental health in, 134
 promoting leadership in well-being in, 135
 radical ideas for, 137–138
 redefining legal workspaces in, 135
Legal organizations, cultivating resilience in, 82–86
Loneliness in the legal landscape, 35–36
Love, 63, 101, 113

M
Mantra meditation, 107–108
Maslow's Hierarchy of Human Needs, 40
Massachusetts Bar Association, 4, 34
Meditation, 63, 105–108. *See also* spirituality
Melodrama, 127–128
Mental Health Awareness Month, 134
Mental health crisis
 "always-on" culture and, 25–27
 embracing mental health as priority, 36–40

Mental health crisis *(continued)*
fear of perceived judgment and, 31–33
fear of perceived weakness and, 23–25
fear of professional consequences and, 27–29
high-pressure environment and, 15–16
importance of addressing, 139
lack of education and awareness and, 34–35
loneliness in legal landscape and, 35–36
opening the dialogue on, 134
perfectionism and, 16–21
as silent stigma, 21–35
"suck it up" culture and, 29–31
Mentors, 137–138
Mindfulness, 55, 95–99
Mindlessness, 105
Motivations, 74
versus behavior, 89–90

N
Non-violence, 113–114
Nutrition, 109

O
Overreactions, 67–68
Overwhelm, 13–14
Ownership, taking, 101

P
Paralegals, 86
Parasympathetic nervous system (PNS), 45, 47, 95–99
Peace, 112–113
Pearls, looking for, 58
Peer support groups, 133
People pleasing, 17–18
Perceived weakness, fear of, 23–25
Perfectionism, 8, 16–21
letting go of, 55
Personal goals, 114–115
Perspective, 8
Persuasion, 59–60
Physical health, 108–109
Pig-headedness, 59–60, 129–130
Platform, finding your, 75
Post-traumatic stress disorder (PTSD), 9, 59, 86, 129
secondary, 86
Practice areas, adjustments to, 62
Practice of law, 91–92
Pranayama yoga, 105–106
Prayer. *See* spirituality
Priorities, 74–75
Professional consequences, fear of, 27–29
Purpose, 58

Q
Quitting, importance of not, 76

R
Rapid breath, 105
Rapport, 75
Realistic expectations, 55, 84–85
Red balloon meditation, 107
Regret, 67
Relaxing breath, 105

Resilience, 47, 48
cultivated in legal organizations, 82–86
emotional intelligence and, 69–82
self-care as vital component of, 87–94
strategies for building, 55–69
understanding, 48–54
Results over hours, valuing of, 135
Right conduct, 112
Rigidity, 18
Roosevelt, Theodore, 78

S

Score, keeping, 130–131
Secondary post-traumatic stress disorder (PTSD), 86
Secondary trauma disorder, 32, 86
Secretaries, 86
Self-acceptance, 90–91
managing workload and boundaries in, 94–95
Self-care, 55–56
being like Buddha and, 116–120
dealing with unpleasant lawyers and, 120–123
embracing the journey to, 124–131
Hakalau and, 104
Ho'oponopono and, 100–103
physical health and, 108–109
pillars of, 94–123
power of mindful awareness in, 95–99
redefining success and, 123–124
setting daily goals and, 114–116
spirituality and, 110–114
strength in connections and, 110
vagus nerve and, 103–104
as vital component of resilience, 87–94
Self-compassion, 77
Self-control, 70
Self-criticism, 59, 90
Self-doubt, 73, 77–78
Self-forgiveness, 101–102
Self-reflection, 55
Self-talk, critical, 67
Service, acts of, 61
Shame, 18, 66–68
Silent stigma of mental health issues, 21–35
Singing and vagus nerve, 104
Sleep, 62
Slow breathing, 105
SMART goals, 115–116
Social skills, 71
Social support, 55, 133–134
Space between thoughts meditation, 107
Spirituality, 60, 63, 110–114, 127. *See also* meditation
Stress
chronic, 86
fun and, 57
immune system effects of, 57
imposter syndrome as source of, 18–21
lawyers talking about effects of, 6–7
prevalence of, 3–4
sources of, 12–13

Subconscious mind, 88–92
Success, redefining, 123–124
"Suck it up" culture, 29–31
Suicidal thoughts, 10–11
Sympathetic nervous system (SNS), 45–47, 86

T

Talk therapy, 32, 62
Teamwork, 56–57
Total responsibility concept, 100
Transcendental Meditation, 105
Trauma, 80
  forgetting and/or forgiving past, 59
Trust, lack of, 18
Truth, 111–112

U

Unpleasant lawyers, dealing with, 120–123

V

Vacation and time off, 62, 135
Vagus nerve, 103–104
Vitale, Joe, 100–101
Voice, finding your, 75

W

Walking meditation, 106
Warrior mode, 45–48, 60, 86, 95–99
Well-Being Toolkit for Lawyers and Legal Employers, 137
Wellness, 57
Work-life balance, 25, 45, 94–95
  realistic expectations with, 55
  redefining legal workspaces and, 135
Workload, managing of, 94–95
Worst-case scenario thinking, 19–20, 125

Z

Zero Limits, 100